# THE LOVERS

# THE
# LOVERS

## AFGHANISTAN'S
## ROMEO & JULIET

The True Story of
How They Defied Their Families
and Escaped an Honor Killing

# ROD NORDLAND

*An Imprint of HarperCollinsPublishers*

Persian and Dari poetry and song translations by Bruce Wannell and Sahar Dowlashahi.

HarperCollins books may be purchased for educational, business, or sales promotional use. For information please e-mail the Special Markets Department at SPsales@harpercollins.com.

FIRST EDITION

*Designed by Suet Yee Chong*
*Photographs by Diego Ibarra Sánchez, Mauricio Lima, Andrew Quilty, Jawad Sukhanyar, and Kiana Hayeri*
*Map by Studio E Genevieve, designer Sisi Zhu*

Library of Congress Cataloging-in-Publication Data has been applied for.

ISBN 978-0-06-237882-8 (hardcover)
ISBN 978-0-06-246576-4 (international edition)

16 17 18 19 20    OV/RRD    10 9 8 7 6 5 4 3 2 1

*In memory of my mother,*
*Lorine Elizabeth Nordland*

*With love's light wings did I o'erperch these walls;*
*For stony limits cannot hold love out,*
*And what love can do, that dares love attempt;*
*Therefore thy kinsmen are no stop to me.*

ROMEO AND JULIET, ACT 2, SCENE 2

# CONTENTS

# DRAMATIS PERSONAE

❧

**Zakia,** Ali's lover, third daughter of Zaman and Sabza;
*and*
Mohammad **Ali,** Zakia's lover, third son of Anwar and Chaman.

## THE AHMADIS

Mohammad **Zaman,** Ahmadi family, Kham-e-Kalak village,
father of Zakia;
**Sabza,** his wife, mother of Zakia;
**Gula Khan,** his second son, older brother of Zakia;
**Razak,** his fourth son, youngest brother of Zakia.

## THE SARWARIS

Mohammad **Anwar,** Sarwari family, Surkh Dar village, father of Ali;
**Chaman,** his wife, mother of Ali;
**Bismillah,** his eldest son, brother of Ali;
**Ismatullah,** his second son, brother of Ali;
**Shah Hussein,** his nephew, cousin of Ali.

## OTHERS

**Najeeba** Ahmadi, director, Bamiyan Women's Shelter;
**Fatima** Kazimi, Bamiyan Province director,
Ministry of Women's Affairs;
**Manizha** Naderi, executive director, Women for Afghan Women;
**Shukria** Khaliqi, lawyer, Women for Afghan Women.

## MAP: ON THE RUN IN AFGHANISTAN

Zakia and Ali escaped captivity and eloped, but were hunted by both Afghan police and vengeful family members. They managed to stay one step ahead of their pursuers in the rugged mountains of central Afghanistan, traveling by foot, in cars and buses, and even by air to neighboring Tajikistan. The couple spent their honeymoon in caves and their first anniversary still in hiding.

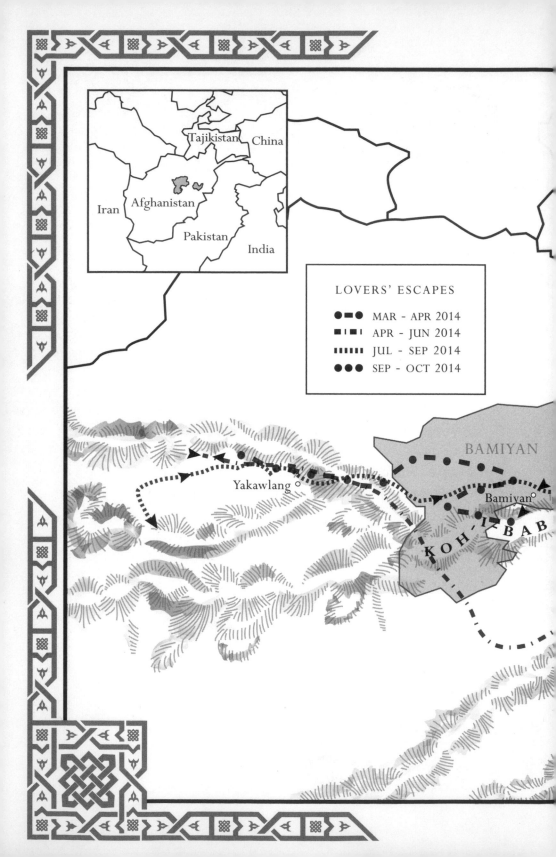

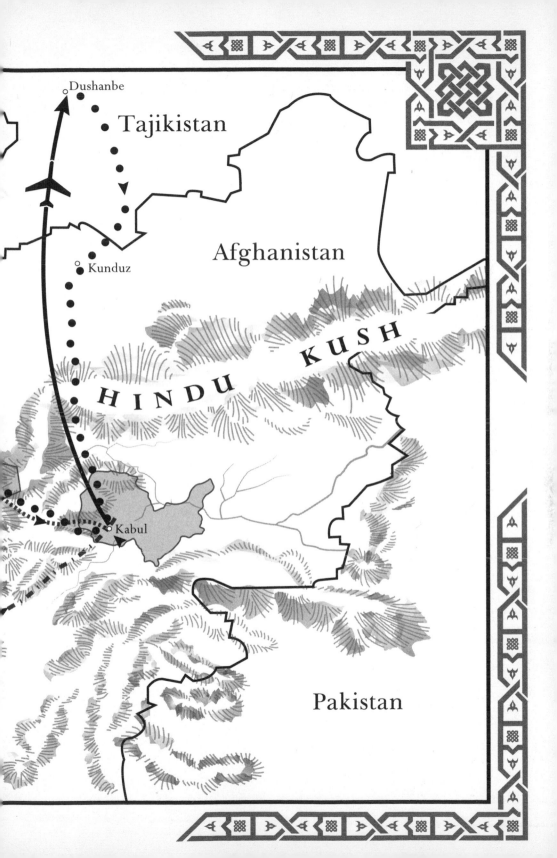

# PROLOGUE

It was a cold clear February day when we finished our first visit to see Afghanistan's most famous young lovers and went out to what passes for an airport in Bamiyan town—a broad cinder runway with a fine view of the cliff niches that once held the Great Buddhas. There was a cyclone fence around a few shipping containers, one of which was the waiting room, another the office of airport management. The United Nations and a private Afghan company, East Horizon Airlines, which had some aging Russian turboprop craft, flew in only a couple of times a week so there wasn't much point in real infrastructure. I remember sitting in the waiting room container next to a *bukhari,* the flimsy, usually rusted stove that burns everything from wood and chips to coal and diesel oil, trying to stay warm as I wrote my first article for the *New York Times* about the lovers. I thought, what a great story, though sad, and with a follow-up that was a death foretold. I expected that the next and final article would be about how the girl's family came one night and dragged her from the shelter or how, out of loneliness and despair or a misguided willingness to believe in her brothers' promises, she would emulate the example of so many other Afghan girls who left shelters to return to their families, believing they'd be safe, and were never seen alive again. We would all be outraged and then turn the page.

That's how such stories usually end, but I was wrong, and theirs was just beginning.

# THE LOVERS

❦

# UNDER THE GAZE OF THE BUDDHAS

Her name was Zakia. Shortly before midnight on the freezing-cold eve of the Persian New Year of 1393 she lay fully clothed on her thin mattress on the concrete floor and considered what she was about to do. She had on all her colorful layers—a long dress with leggings under it, a ragged pink sweater, and a long orange-and-purple scarf—but no coat, because she did not own one. The only thing she did not have on were her four-inch open-toed high heels, since no one would wear shoes indoors in Afghanistan; instead the heels were positioned beside her mattress, neatly left shoe on the left, right on the right, next to the little photograph she had of Ali, the boy she loved. It was not the best escape gear for what she was about to do—climb a wall and run off into the mountains—but it would soon be her wedding day, and she wanted to look good.

That night of March 20, 2014, was not the first time Zakia had contemplated escaping from the Bamiyan Women's Shelter, which had been her home, her refuge, and her prison for the past six months, since the day she ran away from home in the hope of marrying Ali. Always before, her nerve had failed her. Two of the other girls who shared her room were awake as well, but they would make no move unless she did first. Though Zakia was still terrified and did not know if she had the courage to leave, she felt she was fast running out of both time and opportunity.

This was no small thing, although Zakia was then eighteen and legally an adult, a voluntary shelter resident rather than a prisoner, and in the eyes of Afghan law she was free to go whenever she pleased. But the law is only what men make it, and nowhere is that more true than in Afghanistan. What Zakia was about to do would change not only her life and that of Ali, who waited for her call on the other side of the Bamiyan Valley. She understood that it would change the lives of nearly everyone they knew. Her father, Zaman, and her mother, Sabza; her many brothers; and her male first cousins—they would all give up their farm and devote their lives to hunting down Zakia and Ali, publicly vowing to kill them for the crime of being in love. Ali's father, Anwar, would be forced into such debt that his eldest son would lose his inheritance, and most of the family's crops would be forfeited for years to come. Others would be touched in unexpected ways. A woman named Fatima Kazimi, who ran the women's ministry in Bamiyan and had recently saved Zakia from being killed by her family, would flee to exile in Africa. Shmuley Boteach, a rabbi from New Jersey who that night scarcely knew how to pronounce Zakia's name, would end up consumed by her case, lobbying at the highest levels of the United States government to intervene on her behalf. In the course of it all, this illiterate and impoverished girl who did not know her numbers up to ten and had never seen a television set would become the most recognizable female face on the Afghan airwaves. She would become a hero to every young Afghan woman who dreams of marrying the one she loves rather than the one chosen for her by her family, sight unseen. To the conservative elders who preside over their country's patriarchy, however, Zakia would become the fallen woman whose actions threatened the established social order, actions that were yet more evidence of the deplorable interference of foreigners in Afghanistan's traditional culture.

That is where I came in, because the articles[1] I wrote about

Zakia and Ali in the *New York Times* in 2014 would bring them that fame and arouse the ire of the conservative Afghan establishment. I didn't know it at the time, but before long I would become their best hope to survive, entangling myself in their lives in ways that threatened my own values and professional ethics. That night, though, on the eve of the spring equinox and the Persian New Year,[2] I had no idea what they were up to and was three days' travel away from them elsewhere in Afghanistan. We were the last people on one another's minds.

I had visited them in Bamiyan only a month earlier, so when I later heard what had happened, it was easy enough to picture the scene. For some reason the words of the Robert Browning poem "Porphyria's Lover" sprung to mind, perhaps because it was about an impatient lover awaiting the arrival of his beloved:

> The rain set early in to-night,
> The sullen wind was soon awake,
> It tore the elm-tops down for spite,
> And did its worst to vex the lake:
> I listened with heart fit to break.

For elms, substitute the silver birches that are arrayed in proud double rows extending from the southern side of the Bamiyan Valley, where the women's shelter was, along farm lanes cutting down toward the river that runs through it. Tall and slender, the birches are reminiscent of the needle cypresses that flank the lanes of Etruria, except that the silvery backs of their leaves and the mica-like bark all seem to sparkle even in the starlight. Bamiyan town is the capital of the province of the same name, a highland area on the far side of the Hindu Kush mountains, a place of green valleys between barren and forbidding ranges a long way from anywhere. The town is ranged over two broad flatlands on the southern side of the Bamiyan Valley; the lower one holds the ancient town, a collection of mud buildings little different from those there thousands of years ago, interspersed with newer concrete ones, the metal doors on shops in the bazaar painted in primary colors, and, not far below that, the river, still with patches of ice in the middle and snow on its banks.

A few hundred feet higher and farther south, there is the broad plateau that holds the small airport, with its terminal of containers,[3] and a collection of new-build masonry edifices, which were mostly government and aid-group offices. These were constructed by foreign donors along freshly asphalted roads, engineering marvels donated by the Japanese or Korean governments, which are perfectly straight and flat but go nowhere in particular. Among those buildings is the shelter that Zakia was preparing to flee.

Bamiyan town, when it was lucky, would get four hours of electricity a day. There was none at this late hour, so there was no city glare from the darkened town, only the reflected brilliance of the firmament. Earlier in the evening, there was a cold, drizzling rain, but temperatures dropped around midnight and it became a light, windy snow.

The roadside birches promenade from the bottom of the valley up to the elevated plateau, where, even in the dark and at a distance of some two miles from the cliff faces, the niches that once held the Great Buddhas of Bamiyan are impressive. Their huge size and gaping black shapes are at once apparent and on first glance breathtaking, so unlike anything else in the world. The cliffs are just north of the river. The statue of Nelson from Trafalgar Square would be lost within the smaller, eastern niche, where once the Buddha known as Shahmama stood; the larger, western niche that held the Buddha known as Solsal could swallow the Statue of Liberty whole. Ancient craftsmen carved these with hammer, pick, and chisel in a labor of love that lasted lifetimes. Throughout history, Solsal and Shahmama were the two tallest standing Buddhas on the planet.[4] They were fourteen centuries old when they were destroyed over a few days in 2001 by the Taliban, who ranged tanks in front of them and blasted away and then finished them off with high explosive charges.[5] The Taliban rampaged through this valley during their regime, killing the Hazaras who live here by the thousands, motivated by hatred of their race (Asian rather than Caucasian) and their religion (Muslim, but Shiite rather than

Sunni). The Taliban could not, however, destroy the whole vast sandstone cliff, a tawny golden color that reflects well in the darkness and remains an arresting sight. Between and around the niches of the Great Buddhas is a honeycomb of ancient passageways and caves, comprising monks' cells and shrines, some as big inside as the nave of a European basilica, others only a tiny chamber for a long-ago hermit. The cliffs themselves appear to have been flattened by the carvings of ancient hands, to make smooth canvases from which to excavate their shrines, nearly a millennium and a half ago.

All of which is more than just the backdrop to the story of the lovers Zakia and Ali, who as young children fled with their families into the higher mountains when the Taliban came to the valley and who returned after the massacres were over. What happened here long ago, and not so long ago, made these two young people who they are. It shaped not only the destiny that they had defied but also the other one they were on the verge of making on this night when the mountains all around them were struggling to hold on to winter and the Persian New Year was about to begin. In ways odd and thoroughly unexpected, the Taliban had turned Zakia and Ali's entire world on its head and by both their defeat and their bitter resurgence had made the story of these lovers what it would be. Without the Taliban there would have been no Western intervention; without a Western intervention, the story of Zakia and Ali would have been a short tale with a bloody ending.

The warlords who fought the Taliban and later helped form the Afghan government that replaced them were, where women were concerned, as bad as and sometimes worse than the Taliban. Only the insistence of the Western countries on equal rights for women led to a constitution and laws that protected women, at least legally. Culturally was another matter. In recent years, as the Taliban threatened to return to power, Afghan leaders and their Western allies had grown unwilling to expend political capital challenging cultural conservatives on the government side. As a result most gains on behalf of women were made in the early years after the Taliban's fall, with relatively little accomplished once the resurgent

Taliban became a more potent threat after 2012. Western intervention had made it legal for Zakia to choose her own spouse and even to run away with him, but now Western timidity had stranded Afghan women like her in an uncertain limbo of cultural and official hostility.

Zakia was Tajik, and Ali was Hazara; she was Sunni, and he was Shia. Zakia's family was opposed to her marriage on cultural, ethnic, and religious grounds. Now that she had run away, she'd violated another cultural taboo. In Afghan culture a wife is her husband's property; a daughter is her father's property; a sister is her brother's. It is the men in a woman's life who decide whom she will marry, and by running off with someone else Zakia was not just defying their will but stealing what they viewed to be rightfully theirs.

Ali stood outside the earthen wall surrounding the low mud buildings of his family farm compound in the village of Surkh Dar, on the far side of the Bamiyan Valley from the women's shelter that held Zakia. The village was a short way outside Bamiyan town, a few miles past the larger, westernmost of the Buddha niches. Ali was twenty-one then, three years older than Zakia. He stuffed his gloveless hands into the pockets of his faux leather jacket, but it provided little warmth. He, too, was dressed in his finest, getting ready to meet his lover, the woman he hoped soon to make his wife. On his feet were his tan leather shoes with pointy toes, the only pair of footwear he owned besides plastic sandals. If it were not for the holes worn through the sides of their uppers and the caked mud on their soles, these shoes would have seemed more at home on the cobbled lanes of Verona than in the muddy late-winter fields of Bamiyan. Ali stamped the ground, not just to stay warm in the cold and the light freezing rain but because, accustomed as he was to long days of farm labor, any prolonged physical inactivity made him uneasy.

He mulled over how they would greet each other when they finally met for what would be the first time in months, not count-

ing screaming scenes in the Bamiyan provincial courthouse.
Would she call his full name, Mohammad Ali, the sound of which
had always gladdened and surprised him when she whispered it
over the line during the years of clandestine telephone conversations that characterized their early courtship? Zakia was the only
woman, besides his sisters and his mother, he had ever heard speak
his name. Or would she just say *tu,* the familiar "you" in their
language, Dari, a dialect of Farsi or Persian? Three hours earlier
she had called and said this would be the night that she made good
her escape to elope with him and that she would call when she
went over the wall, but it was not the first time she'd said that.
As the hour crawled past midnight and his phone didn't ring, he
began to lose hope. He kept the cell phone next to his heart, in an
inside pocket to protect it from the intermittent freezing drizzle.
A battered old knockoff of a Samsung Galaxy, this cheap Chinese
smartphone full of love songs and recorded birdcalls bore the story
of his life.

One of the songs from their long courtship, which he'd chosen
for tonight's ringtone, played on a continuous loop in his head. It
was from a song by Bashir Wafa, an Afghan pop singer, covering
the story of the Prophet Joseph and Potiphar's wife, who in the
Islamic version of that ancient tale are named Zuleikha and Yousef:

> *If Zuleikha repents, sighing from the bottom of her heart,*
> *Yousef will walk free, the fetters fallen from his ankles . . .* [6]

Sometime after midnight of the Persian New Year, he gave up.
"I thought she must have been kidding with me and had decided
against going through with it," he said. He tried her phone for
perhaps the tenth time, but there was no ring, only the imper-
sonal phone-company message: the same nasal female voice both
in Dari and in English announcing Zakia's phone to be outside the
coverage area. Just in case, he hung his phone on a nail in the wall
outside because the signal in their village was too weak within his
house. Then he went inside to lie down on his bed, like Zakia's a
mattress on the floor, this one of earth. He left the window of his

room open despite the cold so he would be able to hear the phone sing; there was only a wooden shutter without glass, simply a pane of plastic sheeting stretched over the opening, which he slit at the bottom and peeled up just in case.

As Ali went dejectedly to bed, Zakia huddled with her two roommates, Abida and Safoora, across the valley.[7] The three of them had planned to creep out of their beds just before midnight and wait inside the front door of the big house until the guard outside was asleep. The Bamiyan Women's Shelter, run by the UN Women organization with an all-Afghan staff, at that time held fifteen girls and young women like themselves, all there because of the threat of beatings or death from family members or forced marriages to people they could not bear or illegal child marriages or because they were raped. Safoora's case was particularly distressing. Brought to court in a dispute between two families over the terms of her engagement at fourteen years of age, she was taken into a back room at the courthouse and gang-raped by court employees. She complained, but the judges blocked any prosecution of the rapists, and so Safoora was in the shelter fleeing their retribution and fearing her own family's wrath against her. It is commonplace for Afghan families to murder a daughter who has had the poor judgment or bad luck to be raped; the rapist is often treated with shocking leniency. They call it "honor killing." Zakia had fled to this shelter to escape an honor killing as well, though for a different reason.

They say that in the heyday of the Bamiyan Buddhas, when this remote mountain valley was a center of pilgrimage and the spiritual capital of the Greco-Buddhist Kushan Empire, the eyes of the great Buddhas Solsal and Shahmama comprised hundreds of precious stones, rubies and sapphires especially but diamonds and emeralds as well. Fires were kept lit at night behind those yard-wide orbs. The gemstone lenses magnified the light and sent multicolored rays across the valley, where they would have been seen sparkling at night from many miles away, particularly on the upper plateau, which lay at nearly eye level opposite the behemoths' gaze.

Tonight on this same plateau, a male guard was on duty in the courtyard of the women's shelter in a small guard shack that was just big enough for him to lie down inside. The girls knew that he was ill and would probably have fallen asleep on duty, which indeed he had done. Zakia had the SIM card for her cell phone, but the phone itself was in the hallway, hidden in a cupboard. Inside the shelter building, there was a woman guard whom they had expected to be asleep, but she wasn't. The guard challenged Zakia when she heard her stepping outside her room. Zakia quickly ducked into the bathroom, making up a story that she wanted to take a late shower. This delayed her another twenty or thirty minutes as the two other girls waited for her and Ali kept trying unsuccessfully to get through on the phone.

Safoora, younger than Zakia, was excited for her but sad to see her go—she was along just to help Zakia and the other older girl, Abida, escape. Zakia had been not only an older sister to her but also the sparkler that lit up their shabby existence: colorful, vivacious, and, in the privacy of the company of other young women, contemptuous of the social rules that had driven them all to this refuge. Abida, an overweight girl about Zakia's age, married as a child to an abusive husband whose beatings drove her here, had decided the day before that she would flee with Zakia to return to her husband. They agreed to help one another over the wall of the shelter and run together.

It was a shelter from the harm that awaited them outside, but it was also a prison; one of the terms under which all such facilities in Afghanistan operate is that they promise not to allow the girls and women to leave until their cases are settled, if they can be settled. Many of them are in the shelters indefinitely, with few future prospects except to return to whatever family hell drove them there in the first place.

Zakia was determined that would not be her fate. The girls hugged and said their good-byes to Safoora and then began dragging mattresses out to the wall at the back of the courtyard. The mattresses were stiff, full of cotton tick; doubled over and piled one atop the other, they made a ledge halfway up the eight-foot-tall wall, so Zakia could clamber up. Later on she would insist, as she had agreed with the other girls to say, that no one had helped her escape, that she had simply walked out the unlocked front door when everyone was asleep and hopped the wall on her own. From the top of the wall, she reached down to pull Abida up as well, but the girl was too weak to pull herself up and too much deadweight for Zakia. Abida later claimed that her friend had abandoned her to save herself. Zakia insisted that the girl was too heavy to make the climb, but she also was aware that Abida wanted to return to an abusive husband. Zakia thought it was probably just as well that the girl did not do so. Abida was not driven by love but by desperation and might well have been killed for her efforts.

Looking back from the top of the wall for a brief second, Zakia saw that she had let go of Ali's photo on the way up; it had been clutched in her hand and was crumpled badly. She did not hesitate, though, and at about one in the morning Zakia dropped to the ground outside the wall, in her high heels, carrying a plastic bag full of clothes. She ran lightly down the hill in the direction of the Great Buddhas, pursued by a pack of barking dogs, then stopped under some birch trees on a traffic circle at the edge of the upper plateau and dialed Ali. There was no answer. Digging into her bag, frantic, she pulled out a loaf of bread and began breaking off pieces to throw to the dogs to stop the barking.

Over in his village of Surkh Dar, Ali heard the phone ring on its nail outside and raced from his room, but by the time he reached it, the ringing had stopped. He called her back, and this time Zakia answered. Their situation was perilous. It was just past one in the morning, and she was a woman alone and therefore subject to arrest, not only by police but by any man who passed and wanted to take the law into his own hands—or worse. In a society where rape was often not regarded as a crime if the woman were found alone, worse was likely. Ali woke his father, Anwar, to tell him that the escape was on and then called a village friend, Rahmatullah, who had already agreed to help them elope by driving them to a hiding place higher in the mountains.

Rahmatullah's battered maroon Toyota Corolla wouldn't turn over in the cold at first, but the engine finally caught. Ali stamped his foot impatiently as his friend insisted on warming up the engine for a few minutes. The drive was only fifteen or twenty minutes down the unpaved road, along the front of the Buddha niches, through the old bazaar, and up the hill to the higher plateau, where Zakia waited. The sparse grove of birch trees at that spot was too thin to hide her, so she lay prone in a shallow drainage ditch beside the traffic circle. It seemed to Zakia that it took them nearly an hour to arrive, and by then she could see the alarm being raised at the shelter and hear the commotion there as searchers ran around the walls outside, only a few hundred yards from her hiding place. Hunkered down in the ditch, she did not see Ali in Rahmatullah's car as it first arrived, until he alerted her with another phone call.

When the car stopped near her, it set the pack of dogs to barking again, and Ali jumped out to help her put her bag in the trunk. Each spoke the other's name, and in that small way they were—as they both understood—declaring their rebellion against their society's strictures and customs. There are many husbands in Afghanistan who have never used their wives' names, even when addressing them directly. When they address their own wives, often it will not be with the personal "you"—*tu* in Dari[8]—but with the formal you, *shuma,*[9] the same word one would use to address a stranger or an official. They never mention their wives' names in conversation with others. There are many Afghan men who do not know the first names of their best friends' wives. It is considered offensively intrusive to ask men the names of their daughters, let alone their wives.[10]

Ali led Zakia across the muddy lane, she all aswish in her full-length skirt and *chador namaz,* a long, flowing scarf, and he with a lightweight woolen scarf, a *patu,* pulled around his body against the cold but little else for warmth aside from his thin leather jacket. The snow had stopped and the skies cleared, but the moon was new and the night quite dark. As they got into the car, Zakia took his hand in hers and held it tightly. If she had kissed him it would hardly have been more unexpected and only slightly more subversive.

They had been declaring their love for each other for years now in secret and then publicly for the past six months of her effective incarceration in the shelter. They had never been alone together indoors, let alone in the backseat of an automobile. Mostly they had seen each other only in glimpses and clandestine encounters in the fields of their families' adjoining farms and on one day when they were taken to have their case heard in court. Zakia's death sentence was decreed that day in court: implicitly by her judges and in screamed imprecations by her mother, father, and brothers. For two and a half years before that, they had managed to find glimpses of each other and some stolen minutes together on the farm and along village lanes and footpaths, and they had managed to speak many, many times by telephone. Ever since she entered the shelter six months earlier, however, even telephone calls were difficult; phones were forbidden to the girls. Zakia and Ali had been able to meet, with chaperones, only once during that time. Now here they were holding hands.

It may sound like a small thing, but people who had never heard their parents address each other by name, have certainly never seen them hold hands, even in private, let alone in a public place. Courtship even among engaged couples is usually forbidden. Modernized Afghan families might allow a fiancé and fiancée to meet, but only strictly chaperoned and never alone, and not with any sort of physical contact; more often the couple first meet on their wedding night. Both the wedding ceremony and the accompanying celebration are nearly always segregated by gender. Afghan soldiers often hold hands. Children hold hands. Young Afghans of the opposite sex, married or unmarried, in public, never. Where did Zakia get the idea? Neither Zakia nor Ali had ever been to a movie theater—there wasn't a single one in the entire province—and in their villages there was no electricity, let alone television. Although larger villages would sometimes have one shared TV, usually it would be watched only by men, since women were not allowed to attend public gatherings. What gave Zakia the boldness to take his hand in hers? Is holding hands just an innate human impulse? That, like so much else about their story, was a mystery.

Perhaps it was just as simple as this: Having defied one set of grand conventions, to openly and publicly declare her love for Ali and now to elope with him in defiance of her family, her culture, her tribe, and her sect, Zakia was not now going to be bound by any of her society's petty strictures. If she wanted to hold his hand, she would. When I had an occasion to ask her, much later, why she had done so, Zakia's response was this: "Why not?"

Rahmatullah, in the driver's seat, was stunned to see them sit together so intimately. "He was scared, but he's my friend, so he went along," Ali said. The two lovers in the back, finally together after so many months, didn't know what to say to each other. "We hadn't expected this to happen—we didn't really know *what* would happen," Ali said. The pack of dogs surrounded the car and barked furiously as it pulled away. The couple lay down in the backseat as the car passed the shelter and headed out of town.

The escape had been so unexpected that they still had to arrange the next leg of their flight. Two days later, after the Persian New Year's Day holiday, Zakia's court case was to be moved to Kabul. Bamiyan is a mostly Hazara place, so they felt safer there— the courts were dominated by Tajiks who sympathized with Zakia's family, but the police and the governor, the women's ministry, and the majority of the people were Hazaras and could be expected to sympathize with them. That would not be the case in Kabul, they worried; there were many more Tajiks and Pashtuns than Hazaras there. In Kabul, they feared, Zakia could easily be ordered returned to her family, for what would then become the last few days of her life.

Now they were on their way to the home of a distant relative of Ali's in the Foladi Valley, which cut southwest up into the Koh-i-Baba range, rugged, fifteen-thousand-foot-high mountains running from east to west and framing the southern reaches of the Bamiyan Valley. The relative's name was Salman, and Ali's father and his uncle had only just called him as Ali was driving off to get Zakia; now Ali called him from the car. Salman was reluctant at first, partly because he shared his home with four brothers and he would have to get the fugitives inside without the brothers seeing Zakia.

"Why did you do this?" Salman said.

"It happened, and now that it happened, we can't take it back," Ali said. "This happened, and we're with her, and we're escaping."

They arrived in Foladi at Salman's house around the time of the first call to prayer, the *subh,* when the mullah begins chanting over the loudspeakers in the minarets at the first sign of dawn, which at that time of year was about five in the morning. It was easy enough to hide Zakia; Salman led her into the women's quarters in his part of the house, a compound with several separate mud-walled buildings, one for each of the brothers. Only his wife and young daughters were there, and no male but he could enter. Ali could not go there; staying with his wife-to-be prior to marriage would itself be considered a crime, and hiding Ali elsewhere in the house was much more difficult with so many brothers and their families around. So after a hurried breakfast of bread and tea, Salman and Ali headed out, trudging through a foot and a half of snow, up the flank of the mountain, for the ninety-minute hike to the village of Koh-Sadat.

Elders from Koh-Sadat met them outside the first house in their village; the elders had been watching them climb for the past quarter hour. In so much of this barren, treeless landscape, it was nearly impossible to hide even from watchers miles away. "We have come to buy donkeys," Ali said. Koh-Sadat was locally famous for its donkeys, so it wasn't an implausible excuse. For the rest of the morning, they saw one donkey after another. This one was too small, and that one was too old, and the other was okay but too expensive. By then it was time for lunch, and no one can visit an Afghan community without being invited to lunch. They dragged that out as long as they could, the men sitting cross-legged on the mud floor, picking off small pieces of bread to scoop from the communal plate of pilaf and talking about whatever subject occurred to them.

Finally, in late afternoon, they left with apologies and excuses but no donkey and trudged back down to Foladi and Salman's house. "We drove them crazy with our donkey bargaining," Ali said, sharing a laugh with Salman.

By the time they got back, Ali's father, Anwar, had come and a mullah named Baba Khalili had driven in over the Koh-i-Baba mountains from neighboring Wardak Province to marry them. One of Ali's brothers and his cousin Salman would be the witnesses as they tied the *neka:* the signing of a document agreeing on the terms of the marriage and noting the requisite two male witnesses and the mullah who presided (significantly, the bride need not be present, and often is not). Because all of them, save the mullah, were illiterate, they would dampen their thumbs on an ink pad and press them to the paper in lieu of signatures. The *neka* would specify that Zakia, daughter of Zaman of Kham-e-Kalak village, would receive in the marriage a hundred thousand afghanis (about eighteen hundred U.S. dollars at the time) and a *jreeb* of land (about half an acre), from Ali's family. Normally such a payment would go to her *father* as a bride price, although formally it would be deeded to the woman, since a bride price is officially illegal. Sometimes a small portion would be used to buy jewelry for the woman, but that was at the father's discretion. Zakia's father was not present and in no position to collect the hundred thousand afghanis, which was just as well, because Ali and his father were in no position to pay.

Mullah Baba Khalili demanded thirty thousand afghanis to tie the *neka,* formalizing it with the reading of Koranic verses and his signature and stamp. It was a huge sum for such a service, some five hundred fifty dollars, but the mullah was performing the ceremony without the customary presence of the girl's father—and without asking too many questions. "If I don't tie this *neka,* no one will ever tie it," the mullah told Anwar when he balked at the price. The reputation of mullahs for greed is legendary in Afghanistan, one of the reasons they are the butt of many jokes in an otherwise devout land.[11] "If anyone ever challenges it, I will testify for you," the mullah told him.

The young couple spent their wedding night in the unfinished loft of Salman's home, a low-ceilinged, thirty-foot-long room with no stove; it was far too cold for consummation. "It was a long time before we had a real wedding night," Ali said. "We were so cold all we could do was hold each other for warmth."

The next day they moved on, traveling this time in a taxi that

Anwar had arranged and brought for them from Bamiyan town, a couple thousand feet below. They were heading farther up the Foladi Valley as it climbed toward the highest peak in the Koh-i-Baba range, the Shah Foladi, sixteen thousand feet high. Partway up they were welcomed into the home of a distant relative, Sayed Akhlaqi. This time they could travel together openly because they were now married, but they were still foolishly raising eyebrows, even among those friendly to them, by holding hands.

Their stay was short-lived; the next day Sayed Akhlaqi's son raced up the road from Bamiyan on a mud-splattered dirt bike, breathlessly reporting that the police knew they were in Foladi and were on their way. The son worked as a servant in a government building and had heard the police making the arrangements, urged on by Zakia's enraged family members. The police would arrive by evening, and it was already nearly sunset. The couple and Anwar piled into the taxi and headed farther up the mountain. As they climbed the switchbacks, Ali's phone rang; it was someone from down below alerting them that the police had already left Sayed Akhlaqi's house and would probably catch up to them soon. Looking back, they could see the dust being raised on the lower road by the big, forest green Ford Ranger police pickup truck as it climbed toward them. The bedraggled old taxi had no hope of outrunning it, so they stopped at a glade of small trees and heavy brush, where a creek cut across the road. The newlyweds fled into the brush along the creek on the downstream side of the road while Ali's father, Anwar, went the opposite way, on the upstream side, hoping, if seen, to draw the police's attention from the lovers. The driver carried on, but the police truck soon caught up to him. He refused to give them away and denied having had them along—although there weren't many fares on this lonely road toward the Shah Foladi peak. His story was that he had been on his way to pick someone up but never found the person.

Zakia and Ali hid deep in the bushes, he behind a log and she lying down in the wet streambed nearby. "The driver protected us. He said he was looking for us, too, and hadn't been able to find us." The policemen worked their way back down the hill, stopping and shining their truck's searchlight into the brush. "I don't know how they didn't see us," Zakia said. "It seemed like the light was right on us." At length the police escorted the taxi back down the mountain, holding the driver overnight for questioning before letting him go.

For a while the couple searched for Anwar but had no idea where he was; he searched for them as well, equally fruitlessly. It was inky dark, and no one had flashlights. Ali and Zakia began to walk up the mountain, skirting but staying off the road. They trudged, wet and freezing, through the snow, and then at times through slush brought by a fitful rain, until six hours later they reached one of the lower summits of Shah Foladi. Zakia had to take off her heels after they broke and walk in her bare feet.

Between them, to stay warm, they had only two thin woolen *patus*—Sayed Akhlaqi had given them a second one—which became both blankets and coats for them. The batteries on both their phones were nearly dead, but from the top of the mountain Zakia managed to get off one call to Ali's uncle. "We're lost. Can you tell us where we are?" she said. He wasn't able to help them find their way out, but he did understand from what they said where they were and said he would send help at daybreak.

That night they were too tired even to gather firewood and slept rough on the cold, wet ground, huddled in the *patus*. "We weren't so tired that we weren't happy. We were so happy to be together. We had each other," Ali said.

Zakia was less romantic about it. "I was just cold and scared," she said.

By the next day, they reached another false summit. "We thought we were dead, but we kept climbing. My uncle had said to meet at the top of the mountain, and when we got there, we heard some people, and I shouted 'Sattar!' but no one answered," Ali said. Sattar was his uncle's son, and when he did not reply, they thought the men up there must have been pursuers searching for them, so they hid until the voices receded. Finally they found Azhdar village, a place Ali remembered from going partridge hunting with his brothers and his father; from there a trail went back down to his own village, skirting the Bamiyan Valley. It would be fifteen miles of rugged terrain to cross, but it would take them away from the dangerously cold heights of the Shah Foladi.

The second night they slept outside again but were able to gather firewood to stay warm, and the next day they reached the outskirts of Ali's own village of Surkh Dar. Even then they waited two days, sleeping in monks' caves carved into the soft sandstone of the cliff faces, just a ways up the hill. "They didn't find us, even though the entire police department of one province was looking for us," Ali said.

When they finally made contact with Anwar, early on the fifth night of their marriage, the old man was back in their village; it had taken him two days to find his way off the mountain himself. Anwar arranged for Ali and Zakia to stay with a member of the provincial council who had a home in their village. It was just in time; by then the police had become convinced that the couple could have survived only by coming back to Surkh Dar and hiding there somewhere, so they began searching house by house.

"They even hired women who didn't get along with our women to go into the houses to look for us," Ali said. The couple was safely in the home of that friendly Hazara council member nearby. No one dared ask to enter a councilman's house; it was too much of a stretch to suspect that he would have sheltered these farm kids on their elopement. So for the next week they hid only a few hundred yards from the home of Zakia's own family.

Their two families lived on either side of the highway leading to the west from Bamiyan town and the Great Buddha cliffs, toward Band-e Amir Lakes; her family was in Kham-e-Kalak, the lower village, on the downhill side of the highway toward the Bamiyan River. That village was mostly Tajik families, forty or fifty of them. Zakia was one of eleven children, seven girls and four boys, ranging in age from five to twenty-five. Ali was one of eight, five brothers and three sisters. No one in either of their families had ever been to more than a few years of school, and only a couple of them could read or write at all. They were poor farmers, somewhat better off than subsistence farmers but only barely, with small plots of land on which they raised potatoes as a cash crop and wheat and vegetables to feed themselves. Surkh Dar was the upper village, above the highway, where Hazaras dwelled in much poorer homes, made of mud wattle rather than mud bricks or masonry as in Kham-e-Kalak. Ali's large family shared four mostly windowless rooms facing a barren courtyard. Some of the mud houses were built into ledges and slopes, almost like caves. Among these was a complicated, organic network of narrow lanes, many of them barely wide enough for a mule. The dwellings were close to the highway, while their fields were closer to the river, often some distance from the farmers' homes. So it happened that the fields of Ali's father, Anwar, and those of Zakia's father, Zaman, lay side by side in the bottomland along the river. That is where it all had started, some years before.

2

⊷⟡⟋⊷

# DEAD FATHER'S DAUGHTER

The past can be your real destiny, and theirs was messy. Both Zakia and Ali were too young to remember when the Taliban came over the Shibar Pass through the Hindu Kush mountains and into the Bamiyan Valley in 1998. By that point, two years into its conquest of Afghanistan, the Taliban were used to winning ground. They held all of central, western, and southern Afghanistan and most of the north, with the exception of areas controlled by the forces of Ahmad Shah Massoud and his alliance, in the far north, and by Hezb-i-Wahdat, the Hazara militia, in the north-central highlands of Bamiyan Province and Hazárajat.[1] There was no love lost between Massoud's Tajiks and Hezb-i-Wahdat's Hazaras, partly because Massoud's forces had carried out a notorious massacre of Hazaras in Kabul during the civil war a few years earlier and partly because the dominant Hazaras had abused the Tajik minority in Bamiyan city. The Hazaras initially beat back the Taliban in 1998. Abandoned by the more numerous and more powerful Tajiks, however, the Hazaras in Bamiyan succumbed when the Taliban returned in force the following year, carrying out massacres in Bamiyan city and in the Yakawlang Valley in which they killed every male they could find older than thirteen.

Both their families fled the valley during that time. First Zakia's Tajik family headed north to Baghlan Province to flee the Hazaras and the Taliban, and then Ali's family fled to the Koh-i-Baba mountain heights and across into Wardak Province to the south, escaping both the Pashtun Taliban and the Tajiks. There had always been religious tensions between Afghanistan's Sunnis, who include Tajiks, Uzbeks, and Pashtun ethnic groupings, and its Shia, who are mostly Hazara. The Taliban's extremist Deobandi version of Islam decreed that all Shia were heretics and justified killing them, a view they shared with Al-Qaeda. There was also a racial aspect to the conflict, since Hazaras are more Asian in appearance while Tajiks and Pashtuns are more Caucasian, although there are many exceptions. Tajiks and Pashtuns have traditionally derided Hazaras as outsiders, seeing them as the descendants of Genghis Khan's invading armies of eight hundred years ago;[2] Hazaras have never forgiven the Pashtuns for enslaving them in the nineteenth century.

After the Taliban conquest of the province, Hazara and Tajik families with young children began to return to their homes, without their men, particularly families whose children were too young to be viewed as fighters, which was the case with the families of Zakia and Ali. Ali is just old enough to remember the last couple years of the Taliban regime and its occupation of the Bamiyan Valley; in 2001, their last year in power, he would have been seven or eight. His older brothers and father were old enough to be considered fighters, so they fled; he stayed with the women at home. "They were treating Shia people badly, even the children," Ali said. "If you were not Shia, you were not treated badly, but even the chicken of a Shia was treated badly."

With the American-led invasion, the Taliban withdrew and the men came back down from the mountains. Ali remembers that as his childhood's happiest time. "My father and brothers came home, and we thought we were reborn then. Even now when my father calls me on the phone sometimes, he remembers that time and cries, 'How can you be away from me for so long?'"

Zakia's family suffered less from the Taliban occupation since they were Sunni Muslims, but her paternal grandfather, Ali Ahmad, had a difficult time during the great Bamiyan drought. Beginning during the latter years of the reign of King Zahir Shah, just before the beginning of the Soviet occupation in 1979, the drought continued through the civil-war years that followed in the eighties and nineties. Bamiyan is a high desert. Agriculture there depends mostly on snowmelt from the mountain ranges that encircle the Bamiyan Valley, and in those days there were no hydraulic works or reservoirs that the farmers could depend upon. Ali Ahmad fell into debt and sold off his fields one by one, until all he had left to pass on to his son Zaman, Zakia's father, was a house and compound in Kham-e-Kalak village—a substantial place by local standards, with doors and glass windows set into the mud-brick walls—and an adjoining small garden patch, half a *jreeb,* about a quarter acre, which went to Zaman's brother. By the time Zakia was growing up, Zaman had been reduced to sharecropping, working fields rented from more prosperous neighbors, and paying his brother to be allowed to use the walled garden patch next to the house.

Ali's father, Anwar, was luckier. Of his modest ten *jreebs* of land (about five acres), six were well watered enough for his crops to survive the drought years, so he never had to sell his land. The Hazara villagers in Surkh Dar generally were worse off than their Tajik neighbors in Kham-e-Kalak down below. Anwar's family was house-poor, and to this day they have little more than mud shacks to live in. But thanks to the vagaries of the region's ancient irrigation system, they survived the drought better than most and were more prosperous than Zakia's family. Anwar was able to spare three of his sons from farmwork so they could go to a few years of school. In Zakia's family only her youngest brother, Razak, who was age nine in 2014, attended any school. Anwar remained in the shabby mud huts, arranged facing a courtyard that did not even have a wall all the way around it as most rural Afghan homes do. But whatever surpluses there were from potato farming he invested in his children's education.[3]

Zakia would see other village girls, especially among the Hazara in Surkh Dar, the upper village, heading off to school in their blue tunics and white head scarves; the Hazara, so long an underclass in Afghanistan, put a great deal of store in education and were early and enthusiastic adopters of girls' schools when they were restarted in Afghanistan after the Western intervention in 2001. When Zakia asked her father if she, too, could go, his answer was, "No, we're too poor." Instead, like her siblings, she was put to work in the fields, bringing in harvests, plucking weeds, gathering hay as fodder for the animals, and tending sheep as they foraged.

When she was a young girl, Zakia's playmates were not her sisters but her brothers; she was the ringleader and the doll maker. Childhood was a happy time, and on the Eid holidays Zakia and the other kids, boys and girls, would go down to the river and try to catch the little fish they saw there in the crystal-clear pools. Gender differences did not matter when they were young. She taught her brothers how to make dolls from rags and straw, string and bits of stick. "We were all close friends then, my brothers and sisters. The happiest times were when there were wedding parties and we could run around having fun on both sides." Unlike adults, children could go to either the male or the female side of the segregated wedding parties, where there was much dancing, although never between the sexes; in their poor community, no one ever had weddings in a hall but used their homes instead, nonetheless strictly separating everyone by gender.

"When we were young, we were all intimate and friendly with one another, but later on, when we grew up, my brothers got so hard with me," she said. That's commonplace in Afghan families; the brothers are often the most enthusiastic enforcers of their sisters' chastity, partly because the family's honor affects their own marriage prospects and possibly sometimes in guilty response to the sexual tension that can exist between siblings of the opposite sex growing up in close quarters. "My brothers had more control over me than my father did. Whenever they saw me, they would ask me to go inside or to hide myself from strangers, ask me to wear a bigger scarf to cover myself. If I went shopping, they would force me to wear the burqa, which I hated."

When I was able to interview her months later while she and Ali were in hiding, Zakia, who usually came across as the properly shy, self-effacing young Afghan woman, would change when recalling those years. "I hated the burqa before, and I hated it then, and I hate it now. It was really something designed to punish women." Made of a rubbery synthetic material, the classic blue Afghan burqa is a heavy garment, deliberately shapeless, with a mesh grille over a small part of the face to allow some air and vision; it is hot and extremely uncomfortable, many times more unpleasant to wear than an Iranian chador or an Arab *abaya*. Some Afghan men insist, in the absence of any theological evidence, that it is a religiously sanctified garment.[4]

Aside from his friendship with the girl from the Tajik village on the other side of the road, childhood was a lonely time for Ali. His older brothers tended to their studies or did serious fieldwork, like digging irrigation channels; he watched the sheep. At one point in the drama that later unfolded over his love affair with Zakia, Ali indicated his father, Anwar, a cheery little man with an elfin white beard and an old black-and-silver silk turban, and said, "I intentionally did this to him. Since he deprived me of studying and education, I did this deliberately. He allowed my other brothers to continue their studies—my brother Sharifullah studied to the eleventh grade. I did this to give him a hard time, so he faces difficulties because he sent me to look after sheep instead of to school." Abashed, Anwar smiled crookedly. It was hard to tell how serious the son's joking tirade really was, but his father did not dispute him.

Ali did get a little education when he turned eleven and enrolled in the first grade at the local school. It was a primary school started by a nongovernmental organization—no one in the family remembers the NGO's name—but it is now a government school. "I have one good memory of my school time. I used to love birds a lot when I was a child. One day I was asked by my teacher to stand up and repeat the lesson in front of the class. When I stood up, my quail suddenly flew out of my shirt. Everyone laughed, but the teacher was angry. He said, 'Did you come to study or to play with birds in my class?' I loved birds in those days." He stayed through the third grade—some of his classmates from back then were just graduating in 2014 from grade twelve. He studied Dari, math, and drawing but retained little of it; he still cannot sign his name, for instance, although he is adept at dialing a telephone and recites the numbers from one through nine, followed by zero, in the order in which they're arranged on a telephone keypad.

Religious education at the local mosque wasn't much better; he attended for one year. While like most Afghans he describes himself as devout, Ali did not get his piety from his mullah's classes. "The mullah was always beating me, a lot, so I could not learn well."

The year before he entered school, Ali attended a wedding party. Someone had set up a big screen outside, and they were playing a movie on it, an Indian movie dubbed in Dari, *Layla and Majnoon*. He had never seen a movie before, on screen or on TV. He was too young, he said, even to know what love was but found himself watching it spellbound, sitting cross-legged on the ground with the other kids. The name Majnoon is variously translated as "the possessed one" and "the madman"—the word means "crazy person" in Arabic, and it is originally an Arabian tale. Majnoon's madness or single-mindedness is at the heart of all the many versions of the story. Knowing Layla from a young age, Majnoon begins reciting poetry in her honor, obsessively and incessantly; in some versions of the story, that madness itself is his downfall as it turns her father against him, but in other versions he was doomed anyway by lower birth or social and economic differences that made him unacceptable to her father. Then, when Majnoon dies, of course Layla dies as well, of a broken heart. "I didn't understand love when I saw it, but something attracted me to that movie," Ali said.

After Ali quit school, he was sent to take his family's sheep to the higher grazing lands on the sides of the mountains. "We used to go into the mountains to collect sticks for firewood, and on the way there or coming back I would recite poems loudly to the other boys," he said. They laughed at him. "They would tell me, 'You're crazy, you've gone mad,' and I would stop, but after a while they would ask me to recite some more, and I would say, 'No, I'm crazy,' and they would beg me, and I would." Around then an older village boy taught him how to play the Afghan flute, a simple bronze tube with six holes, and he played it a lot, "when I was lonely and to get relief from the pain," he said. That is also when he got to know Zakia-*jan,* as he refers to her; the *-jan* suffix is a term of friendship or endearment, used by males and females, perhaps best translated as "-dear."

Watching the sheep, they played together as their animals foraged sometimes miles from their homes. She was attracted to this moody older boy with his flute, but as a child acolyte, nothing more. She was his only audience; he rarely played his flute except when alone or out in the high pastures with Zakia. Zakia's family had ten sheep; Ali's had twenty-five. "As children we would go to the desert and take our animals for foraging, and we used to spend our days in the huts around.the animals," he said, but they were small children then, too young to think of love affairs. "At that time we didn't even know of these things," he said.

Then Zakia started to reach puberty, and since Ali was three years older than she, there were propriety issues—she was biologically a woman, and therefore by Afghan custom she had to be separated from all adult males other than her brothers and her father. Her family started keeping her indoors except when there was work to do, and then they made sure she was in the company of her siblings. Ali's own father sold their sheep, so Ali no longer had a reason to find her in the privacy of the high pastures.

Some time went by and, as Ali put it euphemistically, he started thinking of her in that way. He was setting out traps for quail, on the still-unplanted fields one day in early spring, and she was in the next field watching him. He has trouble articulating why that mattered, but perhaps there was something in the possibility that his private passion for birds could be shared with someone else. Or perhaps it was just that he would then have been seventeen, and she had turned fourteen.

Ali himself marks the moment when he decided that he was in love to a day when both of their families were in adjoining fields and, as the two families would often do in those days, helping one another with their work. He and his brother borrowed two donkeys from Zakia's family to haul sacks of rocks off the fields, and they chose to ride them back, somewhat scandalously; in Bamiyan a donkey's back should be reserved for work, not pleasure.

"Death to your fathers!" Zakia declared when she saw them. "You use our donkeys to do your work, and then you think you can ride them, too? Curses on you!" Ali and his brother were so startled by the young girl's invective that they both leaped off the animals, laughing nervously. "I think that's when I knew," he said, though he couldn't really say why. Then a few days later, when he found her alone for a moment, he whispered to her, "I love you." He was just trying the words out and wasn't all that sure of his feelings. She ignored him, but she also didn't curse him for his temerity, and he said, "From that time I was forty percent sure of her."

They began to meet and chat more and more often on the crooked paths through the fields, sometimes even managing to meet twice a day. After a while Ali realized that this was the real thing. "I knew I was in love with her." It wasn't just the birds; it wasn't just their ages; it wasn't all the long hours they had spent alone together as children tending the sheep and growing up, but perhaps it was a little bit of all those things.

From time to time, Ali would spot Zakia crossing the fields, and catch her glancing his way, and notice how she would start when he came into sight and alter her course to pass near him as often as she could. By then, as he put it, he was a hundred percent sure about how she felt. It was rare that he could manage to see her for more than a few moments without arousing suspicion, and then she would often be in the company of her younger siblings. "For one month I was searching for her after I fell in love with her, and I knew she loved me, but I didn't know if she would agree to get married to me."

Finally one day he found her alone with no one else in earshot, and he decided to make his move while he could, "quickly because we couldn't stay there long."

They were both working, weeding in fields that were on either side of a mud wall, three feet high, pretending to be absorbed with what they were doing; several of Zakia's younger siblings were playing or working not far away. "I would have gone down on my knees"—he had heard somewhere that was how romantics did it—"but her brothers and sisters were all around and the wall was between us." Instead he blurted out his intentions. "I love you, and I want to marry you," he said, not looking directly at her for more than a moment.

She did not look at him either, not even a glance. "It's not possible. We're from two different ethnic groups, two different religions. No one would ever allow it," she said. Zakia struck Ali as eminently sensible, beyond her years—she would have been about fifteen then, he eighteen.

"We could run away if our families did not agree," he said.

"Then we would have no families," she replied. "We cannot."

He was crushed. "She rejected me, saying that she was from a different ethnic group and such marriages have not taken place before, so it would not be possible. She swore that the relationship was not going to happen. It was really a no, and I was disillusioned."

Zakia was surprised and realized she ought to be offended by his effrontery. "He was very naughty, Ali, and very clever, trying to turn my head when I was so young," Zakia said. "Proposing was very naughty of him. I said we were too young, but it was also the ethnic and religious differences, not just the age. I told him that." Despite her rejection of him, Zakia started thinking about him in a serious way for the first time. Every day she played his proposal over in her mind, every day for a month until she finally decided to seek him out. As she remembers it, her rejection of him was not as final and definitive as it had appeared to him.

Ali mooned around the village all that month, taking pains to avoid places where he might see her, and then, like many a lovelorn young man before him, he decided to join the army. He had no job prospects and no money, and he hated farmwork; Zakia wouldn't marry him, and the Taliban were an enemy that every Hazara could hate. His friends were all joining, including one of Zakia's brothers.

Others from their village who had already signed up said they were assured that they would be stationed somewhere in the west of the country, where fighting was relatively rare in those days. For doing nothing the pay was pretty good by rural Afghan standards, about two hundred fifty dollars a month, and he ended up in the western province of Farah, remote, quiet, and safe.

The boldness of Ali's proposal and his sincerity had touched Zakia's heart, and she realized that she was falling in love with him, too. By the time she'd decided to tell him this, however, he had enlisted and moved away. "I was upset when I heard that he joined the army, since I thought it was because I gave him a 'no' answer, and I didn't want him to join for that reason," Zakia said. Now she wanted to discuss it more, and he was absent. The longer he was absent, the stronger her feelings became.

Ali's army duty in Farah exposed him to the great Persian love stories to a greater degree than ever, as for the first time he was among young men who had smartphones with movies on them, or little DVD players, so popular among troops. Whenever he could, he immersed himself in these bittersweet stories; he felt he knew a thing or two about tragic love.

"Movies? I had never seen any. TV in the village? In the name of God, no, nothing like that in the village, but in the army I would watch some clips on my phone. My friends, some of them had computers, and they would have clips they would share with me." One of those soldiers knew how to transfer video from a computer onto his cell phone, and in this way Ali watched a long TV serial of the Yousef and Zuleikha story. Mostly, though, he was drawn to music clips, and so many of them were love songs. "Music is like a solace to pain. To people who are in love, it is a balm," he said.

In her adolescence Zakia also learned the Persian love stories, not from movies or music—they had only a small transistor radio at home, and mostly her parents played religious programs—but from other girls. The stories were passed around in secrecy among girls who had learned them from older sisters.

"Girls my age would tell them to one another, never openly. It was a secret we all shared," she said.

"There is a clash that exists in Afghan society about love," says poet Jawed Farhad, who teaches Persian literature at a Kabul university and writes love poems that provoke mullahs, with lines like these:

> *I am not an extremist,*
> *Just a great romantic.*
> *So why try to impose your harsh laws*
> *On my affairs of the heart?*[5]

"According to shariah law and the mullahs, romantic love is forbidden, and falling in love without the consent of the family is wrong," Mr. Farhad says. Despite clerical disapproval, people keep the ancient love stories alive; their great antiquity and their roots in religious literature make them on some level impregnable to serious attack. "The mullahs can try, but they can never really suppress them. All those hindrances to love—class differences, economic differences, family differences, religious and sectarian differences, ethnic differences—love is something that does not understand these things. It can cross all these borders, overcome all those differences."

For all the efforts of the mullahs and the patriarchs, Afghanistan has no shortage of love stories; perhaps the official opposition lends them more force and poignancy.

While talking with Afghan scholars about the persistence of the old Persian stories in a culture that is officially anti-romantic, I kept meeting people who would readily admit they were in love. "I myself, I'm in love," declared Ahmad Naser Sarmast, the head of the Afghan National Institute of Music. "I was in love all my life, and I'm proud of that." Dr. Sarmast's school is one of the few truly liberal institutions in the country, with mixed-sex ensembles among the children, aged eight to eighteen, and a coed playground where head scarves are optional and about half the girls do not wear them. "To express our love, we might use symbols, go back to history to find an equivalent. There are so many love stories in this country—no one is going to stop us. Can I deprive my own daughters of love? Being in love is not a crime in any nation. We should give that freedom to our kids. We should give that freedom to this nation."

One of the most popular programs recently on Afghan radio is

called *Night of the Lovers,* which airs weekly on Arman FM Radio
98.1, the country's most popular private station. The format is simple: Young men and women call in anonymously and pour their
hearts out about their loves, usually frustrated, imperiled, or forbidden. They record those personal love stories on the station's voice-
mail system, and the program picks the best ones and airs them.
The idea for the show came to the station's manager, Sameem Sadat,
when he was stuck in traffic one day and saw young people in all the
cars around him happily texting or chatting away, looks of delighted
concentration on their faces. Mostly they were texting even if there
were adults also in the car. Despite being gridlocked for half an hour
or longer, they would keep going without a break. "I realized they
were all in love. No one talks to anyone for thirty minutes or an
hour unless they're in love. I thought, 'They must have stories.'"
The show began on Valentine's Day 2014, at first for an hour once
a week, late at night. It was so popular though that in 2015 Arman
FM increased the format to a three-hour-long program, from 9:00
P.M. to midnight on Wednesdays. After playing each recorded message, the presenters (a man and a woman) match it with an appropri-
ate love song, broadcasting it all without giving any explicit advice
or counseling, to steer clear of the mullahs. After the program the
stories are posted on the program's Facebook page,[6] attracting thousands of comments each week. In a typical week, *Night of the Lovers*
receives three hundred recorded stories from young people all over
Afghanistan, from cities and villages, from educated people and un-
lettered ones, and it broadcasts about twenty of the most articulate.

The stories are nearly always sad. "I would say in all this time[7]
we've had until now ten stories that are happy. Maybe those who
succeed in love don't tell their stories, or maybe there just aren't
many happy stories, I don't know," Mr. Sadat said. The program's
female presenter, Hadiya Hamdard, goes once every few weeks
to Badam Bagh prison for women in Kabul, the country's main
female prison, and collects stories from the inmates there; when
she arrives, she is practically mobbed by women jockeying to tell
their stories. Normally, three-fourths[8] of Badam Bagh's inmates
are there for so-called social or moral crimes, which are of course

crimes of love—sex outside marriage, attempted *zina* (adultery), and so forth. Each episode of *Night of the Lovers* broadcasts one story from a woman who is literally a prisoner of love.

Inevitably, in the messages left with the program, there are sad stories of betrayal and denial, rejection and unrequited yearning. Another leitmotif is how hard it is, in a society that forbids even routine contact between men and women, for lovers to find a way to get together and how easy it is for them to lose each other.

Zakia was in just such a position. With Ali away in the army, she found herself missing him and sorry about turning him down, but there was no way she could communicate her regret to him. She did not have a cell phone, did not know how to use one, and, even if she had, would have had no discreet way to learn his number. Even if she could have found someone to write a letter, there was no mail service in rural Afghanistan. She found herself maneuvering to listen to the men in the family whenever they got calls from brothers and cousins posted in the army, but there was no news about Ali. She felt frustrated and helpless, and as she would come to see it, the powerlessness she felt during those months later drove her to act boldly and take her chances when an opportunity came along again.

Nearly two years of Ali's military service went by, during which he and Zakia had no word of each other. Farah was indeed remote and often without cell-phone service. Once there was a skirmish with the Taliban, and word had trickled back to Kham-e-Kalak. Ali's phone rang, and he was startled to hear Zakia's father's voice; Zaman was calling to find out if his own son, Gula Khan, was okay. Ali was struck dumb for long moments, wanted to ask about Zakia but did not dare, and then assured Zaman that his son was unhurt.

"How is the rest of your family?" he asked Zaman.

"Thanks to God, everyone is fine."

"Everyone?"

"Yes, everyone. What do you mean, boy?"

"That is good. I am glad to hear everyone is fine."

Then one day the Humvee that Ali was in rolled into a ditch, thanks not to the Taliban but to an Afghan National Army driver who, like so many of his comrades, was stoned on hash or opium.[9] The driver had not noticed the small crater in the roadway left by an earlier mine blast. The crash badly fractured Ali's leg. He was shuttled from one hospital to another; it would be nine months before he could walk without pain, and he came home to Surkh Dar to finish his recuperation. That was early in the summer of 2012, a few months into the Persian year 1391.

By then most of the boys who had joined the army from Surkh Dar and Kham-e-Kalak had deserted and returned home as well.[10] Zakia's own brother, Gula Khan, was among the returning deserters, and he related to everyone what had happened to Ali—the only casualty from their neck of the woods. Desperate to see him again, Zakia went to all their usual rendezvous and accidental meeting places, but he was nowhere in the lanes or fields around the village. Ali was lying low, embarrassed about his limp. "I had kind of given up on our love and didn't want to see her then," he said. "Especially with my leg like that."

Finally Zakia saw Ali on the road. She walked up to him boldly and said, "So now it is your turn to avoid me?" There were people around, and she should have been more circumspect, but the words tumbled out; she realized they would have only a couple of minutes to speak without arousing public suspicion, and there was much to say. "You remember what we talked about, what I told you was not possible? Well, now it is possible."

"You see my condition, my broken leg. You wouldn't want me like this. It may never heal correctly," he replied. He does still walk with a slight limp, especially on humid days.

"No, it doesn't matter. It will never matter."

"What are you saying, Zakia-*jan*?"

"I accept your proposal," Zakia told him directly, and then they tried to get away from each other as fast as they could, both appearing as disinterested in the other as possible, as if they had been discussing which well might be best to collect water from. They knew that the moment they aroused any suspicion, their families would intervene to make sure they never found another second alone together.

Ali was so stunned by what had just happened that it wasn't until months after they eloped that he dared to ask her what she had seen in him. When he did, he said to her, "I'm not even that good-looking. What was it that made you love me?"

"You were gentle," she said, "and you spoke to me with kindness."

The next day Ali found a young girl to serve as his messenger and sent a mobile telephone to Zakia, set to silent. All she had to do was answer it, but it soon became clear that she did not know how. He waited impatiently until the moment came when he saw her on the footpaths and could explain to her what to do. "She didn't even know how to drop-call me at first," he said. There was no thought of her dialing his number, because at the time she was innumerate, but he programmed it in for her so it was the only number on her phone. He showed her how to just hit the green button until it dialed and then how to cut it off as soon as it rang on his end, so she did not use up any of the credit on the prepaid SIM card. That would be her signal that it was safe for him to call her back, and all she needed to do when it vibrated was push green again. Never take it off silent, though, he warned her. She had nowhere to plug it in to charge it either; there was no electricity in their house, and if there had been, a phone being charged would be instantly noticed. Many of the little shops and kiosks in such villages would charge a phone's battery for customers for a few afghanis or swap charged batteries for spent ones in popular models. Because a woman would be marked as having a secret affair if she were seen doing that, Ali would charge a spare battery and when they passed in the lanes once every few days, swap it for her old one.

They never fought or quarreled in those days of their secret courtship, until one day when Ali decided to test Zakia's love. Normally Zakia would dial Ali at 8:00 P.M., hang up promptly, and then he would call her back to chat. This time he decided not to, even after she phoned him a second time. On her third effort, he picked up the call and pretended not to know her.

"I found this telephone with this number. Please do not bother me," he told her.

"So you found this telephone and this number?"

"Yes," he said, and she laughed and hung up, expecting him to call back, but he didn't. For several days she did not call him again, and when she finally did, she was angry.

"Why did you do that?" she asked.

"I was trying to see whether you truly love me."

"That was a bad way to do it." Zakia was so angry that she didn't speak to him for another week. When at last she did, he was chastened and promised he'd never play with her affections like that again.

"After that, we never fought or disagreed on anything," Ali said.

Their phone rendezvous were always going to be dangerous, in small homes crowded with many family members. "Once I was on my way up to Qarghanatu in Yakawlang"—a place they would later come to know in their flight—"and it was winter, and snow was everywhere," Ali said. This would have been the winter of 2012–13. "We went to get our family's money from someone who owed us some money. I received a dropped call from Zakia-*jan,* but I did not have credit on my phone to call her back. So I rushed to a shop and put credit on it." That took an hour, by which time Zakia had stopped expecting a return call and had left her phone unattended, forgetting to hide it well. When he called, her brother Gula Khan found the phone and answered it but, suspicious, did not say hello.

"Zakia?" Ali said.

"Who is this?" her brother demanded. Gula Khan had been in the army with Ali, and they knew each other well.

"I'm sorry, I dialed the wrong number," Ali said, hoping Gula Khan wouldn't recognize his voice.

They hung up, but Gula Khan thought he knew the voice, so from his own phone he dialed the number that had just called for Zakia, and when he did, "Mohammad Ali" came up on his screen. Gula Khan could not read and write much, but he could recognize the names stored in his phone.

Gula Khan called Ali back. "Is it Mohammad Ali?"

"Yes."

"Why did you call my sister?"

"By mistake."

Gula Khan did not believe him and yelled at him never to call again. After he hung up, he turned on Zakia, who was three years younger than him. "Gula Khan came and beat me with his hands. He broke my phone, he beat me, he cursed me and warned me not to talk to Ali again," Zakia said. "I didn't mind the beating, but I really hated being cursed."

Before long, Ali had enlisted the same little girl who'd delivered the phone to Zakia, a girl who was not from either of their families, and gave her a few afghanis to carry a small wadded piece of paper to Zakia. On it was written his phone number. Zakia begged some money from her father to buy clothing—it was still a time when he would give her whatever he could, as the prettiest of his daughters. Instead she used the money to buy a cell phone, again through the agency of the girl, who was too young for anyone to suspect that she was doing anything other than carrying out an errand for her parents. The younger girl, who was one of those who went to school, even showed Zakia how to use the phone and how to enter the number Ali had written. Soon they were speaking nearly every evening and managed nearly every day to meet on the footpaths around the village. "Most of the time, it wasn't really an accident that we met," Ali said with a pleased smirk.

One day Zakia had been fiddling with the phone, trying to figure out its mysteries, and had accidentally switched it from "silent" to "normal," without realizing. She drop-called Ali, and he called her back, and to her horror it was really ringing, with her father in the next room. She could not figure out how to quiet it, shook it, tried to pull the battery out, failed, and finally hid it under a cushion. By then Zaman had stormed in and soon found it, still ringing. He threw it against a wall, then took the SIM card out and crushed it. "He just took the phone and cursed me. He didn't beat me. My father never beat me back then. Just my brothers did, mainly Gula Khan."

Her siblings all soon turned on her, she said. "When this matter with Ali happened and they found out about my affair, even my little brothers and sisters tried to distance themselves from me," she

said. "It was very hard. Everyone in my family was against me."
Even nine-year-old Razak, the one she had felt closest to, would
not speak to her.

It took Ali a few days of radio silence to realize what had happened; it was a particularly bitter winter and too cold during that
February and March of 2013 for them to connive to meet in the
lanes and the frozen fields during the day. Instead he resorted to
secretly visiting her home at night. In those days he had taken
a temporary laborer's job at a construction site, working a night
shift that finished at midnight, and he would come over afterward
when the lanes were deserted and the homes all dark. There was
a walled vegetable garden outside the window to Zakia's room,
where Ali would stand and call to her, as quietly as he possibly
could, because she shared the room with the other girls and young
boys of the family. When she heard him, she would steal out of the
house and climb to the flat roof, where she could look down into
the garden and they could talk in whispers. The garden was barren in winter; about a dozen leafless apricot and apple trees lined
the mud-brick walls and surrounded long rows of tilled earth now
frozen hard. In one corner was a pair of ragged bamboo cages in
which Zakia's father kept his partridges—used in the Afghan version of cockfighting—when he could afford them. A small brook
had been diverted to enter a hole at the base of the garden wall, ex-
iting through the opposite wall. Ali's 2:00 or 3:00 A.M. visits to the
garden became regular occurrences, even on the coldest of nights,
but at first she would not come down to join him.

"It was dangerous for both of us, and it was so hard," he said. "I
would wait outside her house sometimes under a rainy sky, sometimes snowing, sometimes so cold she was concerned about me in
the bad weather."

"I was always so frightened we would be caught and so worried
for him," she said. On one particularly cold night, Ali stood in the
garden, dripping wet from a frigid rain that had turned to icy snow,
and recited famous lines from a poem by the twentieth-century
Iranian poet Malek o'Shoara Bahar, which have made their way
into Afghan pop music:

*Love is a nightingale pouring out his heart in song for a rose,*
*Bearing patiently the stinging lacerations of her thorns.*[11]

"I don't read and write, which is why I don't know any real poems by heart," said Ali, "but I love hearing love poems from others and listening to them read by singers." He knew that there was a world out there in which poetry existed independently of music, and he even knew a few verses from famous poems. Songs, however, he knew word for word. Memorizing the words from music was easy, and he did not need to read anything; often he wasn't aware of the lyrics' roots in written poetry, not aware that when he recited lyrics without music, he was simply reciting poetry. They were all verses to him, arrows in his quiver.

Zakia's favorite singer was Mir Maftoon, an Afghan from the mountainous northern province of Badakhshan, a place more remote than Bamiyan. Long before dawn one morning, early in the still-wintry spring, Ali recited one of Maftoon's verses to her as she lay prone on the flat roof of her house, her chin on her folded hands, looking down over the edge:

*Your two dark eyes are those of an Afghan,*
*But the mercy of Islam is not in your heart.*
*Outside your walls I spent nights that became daylights;*
*What kind of sleep is this that you never wake up?*[12]

Touched by the verses and by his suffering in the cold, and freezing herself, Zakia finally came down to join him in the garden. And so their love story became a love affair, as Ali delicately put it. He would have stayed there in spite of the intense cold on those mornings, but come the first call to prayer, the *subh,* which came long before any sign of dawn in these highlands, people would start stirring, going to the mosque to pray or beginning early chores in animal pens and fields. He needed to be well away from her house by then.

"If someone loves someone, she should have that bravery to do whatever has to be done," Zakia said. "For a long time, I was thinking about it and thinking about doing this, and why should I regret it now? That poem moved me, it increased my courage. Those days were so cold, and he was coming to meet me anyway, even though I told him not to come, because the weather was very cold, and he came anyway, and then he recited this poem."

It was only a matter of time before they were caught. Ali slept in the same room with his older brother Ismatullah, and his nocturnal escapades did not escape notice.

"What are you doing?" Ismatullah yelled at him. "I *know* what you are doing, and it's crazy!"

One night Ali went out at 3:00 A.M. to meet her. "Zakia-*jan* and I were in the garden, and we must have stayed too late, because her mother saw us. She didn't recognize me, because at night I would wear different clothes—I wore a hat at night, which I never did during the day." He ran for the far garden wall and scampered over it in a bound.

"Who was out there with you?" Sabza demanded of her daughter, through the window.

Zakia replied that she had woken up early to grind flour and there was a farmer in the garden who begged for bread, so she went out to give him some. It was an unlikely story, and Sabza did not believe her.

"Come back inside, you *dead father's daughter*," Sabza hissed at Zakia. The curse cut deep. Of course her father was still alive, but few things were worse in Afghan society than the suggestion that a daughter might have no father to determine the rest of her life for her.

"I get really upset if someone curses me," Zakia said. "I hate being cursed. After my mother realized I was having a secret affair with someone, she mistreated me like that. I would rather she beat me than curse me." Despite the curses, her mother was at that point being kind. If Sabza suspected that her daughter had consummated her affair, she kept that suspicion to herself—voicing it would have been Zakia's death sentence. It was a serious enough offense just to be discovered showing interest in a boy, far worse to be caught alone with him; the presumption always in such cases would be that sex had taken place. Her mother apparently preferred to present the case to the family as a matter of her suspicions about something starting to go on, or the situation would have become far more perilous for both of the lovers. Also, she had not actually seen who it was, though she knew well enough that it must have been Ali.

With both families alerted and everyone on the lookout, it was even harder for the two young people to get together. It was as if their villages had become prisons, with all their families and neighbors the guards and the two of them the only inmates.

With spring came the new Persian year, 1392, significantly the year in which Zakia would turn eighteen and become legally an adult. Her birthday was unknown, because her national identity card, like those of most Afghans, gave only the year of her birth; so legally she was eighteen the moment it became 1392—March 21, 2013. By that time her father normally would have been shopping her around, hunting for a husband whose family would pay a suitably high bride price. Zakia was considered strikingly beautiful, fair-skinned with hands somehow unroughened by farmwork. Girls in that village were frequently married off earlier than eighteen, and usually the bride price was figured in livestock; four goats or six sheep was a typical sum. Zakia would fetch much more, possibly enough to help Zaman buy some land of his own; he would later claim to have turned down 11 lakhs of afghanis—1.1 million afghanis, or twenty thousand dollars—for her hand. (A lakh is 100,000.) That would be a small herd of sheep or half a *jreeb* of land.

Whom she married was up to her father, and that is not just the case in backward rural areas. It is the predominant practice in all of Afghanistan that fathers rule every aspect of their daughters' lives, even when they are adults. Their fathers decide whether they can go to school, get a job, leave the house, see a doctor, wear a burqa or just a head scarf. Once women are married, their husbands assume that power over them. No one questions male authority over women in Afghanistan. If for some reason the father is absent or the husband dies young, a brother will assume ownership of the woman. Zakia could consider herself lucky that she hadn't been married off at the age of sixteen—the minimum legal age according to both Afghan law and shariah law in Afghanistan—or even at the age of fourteen, a practice that remains widespread although it is forbidden by the constitution and subject to strong penalties under the Elimination of Violence Against Women (EVAW) law.[13] The age at which many girls are married in Afghanistan would be considered criminal sexual abuse in most countries.[14]

Once they had resolved to marry, Ali and Zakia's first instinct was to try to operate within their society's cultural framework. Ali managed to persuade his father to make a bid for Zakia on his behalf. There are exceptions to the practice of fathers choosing their daughters' husbands, but they are shrouded in secrecy, with the goal of maintaining the appearance that the husband was the father's choice. Such exceptions, not talked about openly, do take into account how people really feel and behave. In the traditional model, the wife will never see her husband until their wedding night. In cities and among elites and more progressive families, the families of the prospective bride and groom may arrange for the couple, once the fathers have chosen them, to meet and get to know each other, closely chaperoned; in some cases they will tie the *neka* in advance, so that they're formally married in the eyes of Islam but will not have the wedding party and the wedding night until later. That enables them to court and have intimacy at some level, without committing a legal or religious crime in the eyes of the community. But for the girl or boy to come up with the idea of marrying and then present it to their families openly would be considered shameful. The prospective groom might, however, conspire with his own father to initiate the idea by making overtures to the bride's father, which is what Zakia and Ali tried at first to do.

They were pleasantly surprised by how agreeable Ali's father, Anwar, proved to be about the idea initially.

"By then everyone knew, though no one talked about it publicly," Anwar said. People only had to see Ali walking along the footpaths playing his flute to know that he was in love with someone, and if they also spotted Zakia singing to herself in the fields, as she often did, it wouldn't take long to put the two together. Such interventions are also done behind the scenes in cases where everyone has already begun to suspect that the girl and the boy have somehow found love on their own.

Between the two of them, Ali and Zakia had agreed that they would give it a bit of time, first for the memory to recede of the intercepted telephone conversations and the incident in the garden, and also because Zakia's own brother was about to get married, and after that expense—the groom's family pays for everything, including the bride price—perhaps her father would be more amenable to an arrangement that would help him recoup some of his financial outlays.

"We agreed we would wait two months, but after forty days I couldn't bear it any longer," Ali said. He persuaded his father to make the approach.

The first time the two old men met, late in the summer of 2013, Zaman received Anwar graciously and politely, with green tea and cakes and nuts, dried chickpeas, raisins, and hard candies set out on trays on the floor; they sat facing, cross-legged on thin floor cushions. They had known each other all their lives and been neighbors except for the few years after they had fled in different directions from the Taliban. Their respective fields shared some of the same irrigation channels and works, and they often pooled their labor.

Anwar's opening to Zaman was formulaic, words passed down through generations and known as the *khwast-gari,* the demanding.[15] "Please accept my son as a slave to your family," Anwar said.

Zaman had expected as much and had his answer ready. "I don't want to be harsh, but I tell you that such matches did not take place between two ethnic groups in the past and are not possible now," Zaman replied. "Please, now, do not come again about this."

Anwar hopefully viewed that as a negotiating position, so over the next month he went back twice more, finally offering a portion of his fields—Ali's inheritance—as well as money and gold as the bride price. "You don't have any fields of your own. I can give you fields and money if you want, maybe enough to build a house for one of your sons," Anwar told Zaman.

"I don't care about these things. My relatives and my villagers will get upset with me if I marry her outside her ethnicity and her religion."

Having asked three times, Anwar considered the matter closed. The romance would have to end, and he told his son as much. Their families had been on opposite sides in Afghanistan's bitter civil war, although both had been tormented by the Taliban rule that followed it. But while peace had reigned between Tajiks and Hazaras for more than a decade, memories were long and prejudices died hard. Anwar had no inclination to stir up a war, and he accepted Zaman's right to decide Zakia's fate.

Examples of what was likely to happen if the father's will was defied were abundant. A similar Hazara-Tajik affair had just played out in Bamiyan around the same time Zakia and Ali's courtship had begun, and it was widely publicized. An eighteen-year-old girl named Khadija from Qarawna Village, in Saighan District, had taken refuge in the Bamiyan shelter rather than be married to a man chosen for her by her father. Khadija, a Tajik like Zakia, also had eloped with a Hazara, Mohammad Hadi, but police arrested her after hundreds of other Tajik villagers protested—even though she was of age and had formally married Mr. Hadi. After spending months in the shelter, Khadija got homesick and asked to see her family; with the supervision of Bamiyan's Tajik judges, they assembled elders from their village with the girl's relatives, including her father and her brothers, who all put their thumbprints on a document promising never to harm her. Fatima Kazimi, the head of the women's-affairs ministry in Bamiyan at the time, convened a committee of social workers, shelter officials, and police to discuss the case. The committee opposed Khadija's return to her family but the decision was overruled by the court. Khadija has never been seen since. A few weeks later, when the women's ministry asked to see the girl to make sure she was unharmed, the family calmly announced that she had run away again, Fatima said. This time, though, they showed no interest in pursuing her. In the highlands of Bamiyan, there is really no place a girl alone could run; police would have arrested her on sight. "I'm sure they killed her and hid the body where no one has found it," Fatima said.[16]

Anwar was aware of the stakes, and so was everyone involved. Zakia's family made sure she was more cloistered than ever, and Ali fruitlessly paced the pathways of her village, crossed and recrossed their fields, hoping for a glimpse of her, and tried repeatedly to call her, all to no avail. She was leaving her phone off for fear of being caught with it again. It was so very wrong, Ali felt. "Why should parents choose who we marry? It is not the mother and father who have to spend a life with the woman, it is me. No one can live with his or her mother or father forever. It's the husbands and wives you spend the rest of your life with." He vowed that if he ever had a daughter, he would make sure she could choose her own husband. "I have felt what that was like, and I would never let that happen to anyone."

Zakia drop-called him, and when he called her back, he was nearly in tears. He wanted to tell her the story of Layla and Majnoon. "Ali-*jan,* I know the story," she said. "But tell it to me again."

Layla and Majnoon grow up together, but from different stations in life, and when their childhood love blossoms, Majnoon approaches her father and is rebuffed.[17] He goes mad and wanders the streets of their town, composing and reciting love poetry in her honor until finally Layla is married off by her father, whereupon Majnoon flees into exile and the life of a hermit. She refuses all the advances of her husband, however, and remains chaste throughout their marriage. Layla and Majnoon meet, but they do not consummate their love, and she remains loyal to her nonetheless chaste relationship with her husband. Her husband finally dies, and Layla puts on a bridal gown and plans to join Majnoon at last. By this point Majnoon has wandered off into the desert, mad with grief, and no one can find him. Believing their love to be doomed, Layla dies. Majnoon hears what has happened and rushes to her grave, where he dies as well. They are united in death, and their grave site becomes a place of pilgrimage.

Like the story of Yousef and Zuleikha and another popular tale, that of Princess Shirin and the stonecutter Farhad, the Layla-and-Majnoon story is wildly popular in a society where romantic love is all but outlawed—probably precisely *because* it is outlawed. Yousef and Zuleikha is retold in a thirty-part serial that is played on Afghan television every year during the holy month of Ramadan—in part because, unlike some of the other great Persian tales, it is also a sacred story, enshrined in the Koran, so the mullahs cannot object to it even though it is a story replete with the themes of adultery, romantic love, and the coveting of other men's wives. Afghan popular music, both Westernized pop as well as folkloric versions, and poetry are rooted in traditional romantic tales, particularly these three and their many variants. In a society where the majority of women are in arranged marriages to which they did not consent freely,[18] these songs and poems summon the emotional life they will never have the chance to experience themselves.

Every once in a while, even in Afghanistan, a true love story comes along that echoes those of the past and arouses the whole country. The famous tale of Munira and Farhad in 1991 came at the end of the Communist regime and the beginning of the civil-war period. Kabul was in civil turmoil as the mujahideen battled one another. Rival factions used truck containers as roadblocks and as protection from shelling and gunfire, so the containers were a ubiquitous feature of the cityscape. Munira and Farhad were young people who had fallen in love, but as Sunni and Shia their own union was forbidden. Due to be married to other people on the same Thursday, they arranged to meet secretly one last time the night before, but the only place they could find to be alone was in one of the shipping containers. While they were inside, the owner of the container came along and latched the door from outside. They were too frightened to cry out and be discovered, and by the time the owner opened it again, the oxygen in the container had been depleted, and he found them both dead in each other's arms. Their bereft families, united like the Montagues and Capulets over their shared tragedy, dressed them both for burial in the wedding clothes that had been intended for the arranged marriages that would never take place.

The story fired the imagination of the country and infuriated the mullahs. None of the clerics would agree to preside over their double burial, and instead elders of both families stepped in and performed the funeral rites—under Islam any knowledgeable person can do so.

Neither Zakia nor Ali could have imagined this yet, but their own misadventure would soon be on its way to a similar sort of fame. Munira and Farhad belonged to their parents' generation. A younger generation of Afghans would find in Zakia and Ali's story justification for expressing love openly and proudly, and older Afghans who had loved secretly and guiltily could find vindication, knowing they were not alone.

⤞⟨❧⟩⤝

# 3

# ZAKIA MAKES HER MOVE

When Mohammad Anwar trudged home after a long day tending the fields in the late summer of 2013 and opened his door, Zakia was sitting there on floor cushions and drinking tea with his daughter-in-law.

Anwar's house was a dwelling that shouted poverty but was scrupulously clean—earthen floors swept, carpets shaken and beaten, latrine isolated and limed. The home was made up of four separate rooms, each a little building opposite the courtyard wall. Afghans love walls around their compounds; it is how they keep their women safe from the view of outsiders. Anwar had run out of money for mud bricks, and the wall was only three-quarters complete, with a jagged gap where he hoped one day to install a gate. There was no running water—the nearest water came from a well a few hundred yards away, beside the main road—nor any electricity, save for a tiny lightbulb and wire in one room that could be connected to a nine-volt battery, when they could afford one. The family's two-inch-thick Afghan mattresses were quarter-folded and stacked along the rooms' interior walls during the daytime; bamboo mats or the cheaper plastic mats were used where they could not afford carpets. There was no furniture; thin cushions were scattered around for seating. At mealtimes a plastic sheet was unrolled on the floor to make a dining area, and meals were taken communally, everyone eating from a common plate with their fingers, according to Afghan custom. Like the rest of the dwellings in Surkh Dar village, the homestead was nestled into a narrow valley that rose from the road into the northern mountains; they had used the steep hillside to create the back wall in some of the four rooms. After only a ten-minute climb up the slopes nearby, one could glance back and Anwar's house and the rest of the village would seem to disappear into the landscape, its walls and roofs made of the same earth as the bare slopes all around. Anwar's house was also old, built by his grandfather, and decades of wind and storms had softened all the edges so that it seemed not so much erected as grown in place.

Anwar sat down to tea with Zakia, dazed with surprise. Zakia sat twisting her wrist with the opposite hand, as she often did when nervous, but was otherwise composed. There was already a lot on Anwar's mind those days; harvest time for potatoes, their most important cash crop, was not far away. Prices were good that year, and harvests were likely to be bountiful, although labor-intensive. He might even begin paying down the debts he had incurred with the marriage of his eldest son, Bismillah, several years before, and his next-oldest son, Ismatullah, the year after that. Sons are highly prized in Afghanistan; they are the measure of a man's worth. Though daughters can bring a substantial bride price to their fathers, they are disdained. A man with many sons is considered a rich man no matter how poor it makes him. Anwar had five sons but only three daughters, so he was proud but perennially broke.

Many Afghan men do not even know how many daughters they have; if you ask them how many children in their family, they're likely to reply "five" if they have five sons and five daughters, for instance, since daughters don't count. Press them for the number of daughters and often they will have to consult with a child or a wife to be sure. Anwar, however, is not one of those men.

As if it were the most natural thing in the world, Zakia calmly poured Anwar some tea.

"Why are we here?" he said. "What is this, daughter?" He used the term as an older man addressing a young woman, nothing more.

Things had been coming to a head for months now; it was nearly a year since Ali's return from the army and months since their secret engagement. Zakia was on her third phone, keeping this one hidden in her underclothes after first her brother and then her father found the earlier ones. Although Sabza had not been able to identify Ali that dawn when she caught her daughter with him in the garden, and Ali managed just in time to climb the wall and run off, by then everyone had a pretty good idea with whom Zakia was involved, even if they couldn't prove it. Once Anwar had formally asked for Zakia's hand, it was no longer a secret in either of their villages. "Everyone knew about it. I just made up my mind: I'm not free here at home, so I have to go to him, and I just went," Zakia said. "I just thought about Ali, and I thought, 'I have to go to him.' I was hopeful he would keep me or accept me, but I didn't know. I just had to do it, even if I wasn't planning."

What she didn't say, and could not say, is that she and Ali had become lovers and she had no other choice; there could never be another Afghan husband for her.

She told Anwar that she wanted to see Ali, and that they needed to discuss something with him. Unfortunately, Ali was away working on a day-laborer job some distance from the village and would not be back until Friday.

"I am sorry, daughter. You cannot see him," Anwar said. He pretended not to know what was in the offing, but it was all too clear. Just her presence in the home of another man, even chaperoned by his daughter-in-law, was an outrage to public morality. He walked Zakia halfway home, to the highway that is the boundary between their two villages.

When he came back, he saw neighbors gathered in the lanes, whispering among themselves, and it was clear that word was out and Zakia had been spotted on the wrong side of the highway.

One of Anwar's neighbors came over to talk to him about it, so he decided to preempt the inevitable gossip and telephone Zaman, Zakia's father. One of his sons dialed for him, since he did not know how.

"Your daughter came over to my house, and she may now want to run away with my son," Anwar told him. "It's better that you agree, because if that happens, it will be too late."

"If that happens, I will demand five hundred thousand afghanis, and I know you are in debt already. You're standing looking down the edge of a cliff, and this will put you over it," Zaman replied.

That was an impossible sum, more than nine thousand dollars.

"My debts are not your problem, but if they run away, there will be nothing for you."

Zaman still refused.

Over the next month, Ali and Zakia were rarely able to speak to each other, because Zakia's family watched her so closely. When they did manage to get a few words together, she told him she would come again and that if his family would not take her, they would run away. She said she was now legally an adult and no one could stop her. "We agreed that if Ali's family did not accept this, then we will go somewhere secretly that no one knows—just somewhere, we didn't have any idea where. After the first time I went to their home, I said that they could send me ten times back and still I would come again. It's because I really loved him. I was very determined. I really loved Ali, and my decision was final. It was a strong decision."

The next time she saw an opportunity, she made her move, heading to Ali's uncle's house rather than to his own, thinking to evade pursuers that way. His uncle called Anwar, while Ismatullah restrained Ali from leaving to join her. Ali fought back against his older and much bigger brother, and finally Ismatullah, infuriated, smashed him in the face with a rock to subdue him, leaving a bruise that would take many months to heal. (It was still prominent when I first met Ali the following February.)

Anwar reached his brother's house and confronted Zakia. "You cannot do this," he said. "What are you thinking? Daughter, why are you doing this?"

She pleaded with him openly to take her in to his family so she could marry his son. "We love each other, and we want to marry, and no one should stop us." She was dry-eyed and determined not to cry.

"That is not your decision. It can never be," Anwar said. He took her by the arm and forcibly walked her back to her own home, with two of his sons helping and Ismatullah still holding Ali back from intervening. It was nearly midnight, and the Zaman household was already aroused, aware that Zakia had bolted. Gula Khan was on the rooftop with another brother.

"Let's go before they attack us," Anwar told his sons as they left Zakia in front of her house. "You can see how angry they are."

When he got back home, Anwar, too, beat his son, shouting at him that he was bringing disgrace and humiliation to both his own family and Zakia's. "We didn't want their family to be disgraced," Ali said. Months later part of him agreed with the punishment he received and part of him was still angry about it.

"That night was very bad," Zakia said. The following day was the first day of the main potato harvest, and everyone would have to be in the fields, but the entire family stayed up late screaming at her. "That night my father and my mother both beat me," Zakia said. "It was the first time they had ever done that to me." Gula Khan and her other brothers had always been the enforcers of her virtue. In the course of that parental beating, she finally realized how dire her situation was. "While they were beating me, they were saying, 'We will kill you if you don't listen to us. We have to do this. We have to kill you.'"

The next day both families were in their fields, side by side, both Zakia and Ali bruised. Harvesting potatoes by hand is back-breaking work, and no one spoke across the low mud walls and sometimes just footpaths that separated their two domains. Zakia dared not look at Ali, nor he at her.

No one expected that she would try to bolt again that same

night, but that is what she did. When her family was asleep, exhausted from the day's exertions, she crept out at about 11:00 P.M. and went again to Anwar's home. This time Ali was half expecting her and was still up when she arrived.

"My whole family wanted to send her back," said Ali. "They wouldn't agree. I saw there was no place to go, so I brought her to the women's ministry." It was late at night, but the guards at the ministry building summoned a woman who headed the provincial human-rights office, Aziza Ahmadi, who came down and arranged for Zakia to be admitted to the Bamiyan Women's Shelter, a short distance away.

"I was happy to be in the shelter at first, because I knew that my life was at risk now, and I wanted to see my case handled legally," Zakia said.

She had no idea then, in October 2013, that she would still be there nearly six months later.

At first Zakia cried inconsolably. "She would cry for one or two hours straight, even during late nights," said the shelter director, Najeeba Ahmadi (no relation to Aziza Ahmadi). Other than a small plastic bag of clothing she had brought along to Anwar's house, Zakia's lone possession was the tattered photograph of Ali that she kept beside her thin mattress on the floor. Ali's mother gave it to her when she visited the shelter herself, partly because Chaman wanted to make sure the shelter authorities knew that Ali's family was behind her and partly to reassure and comfort Zakia. Later the police would confiscate the photo from the shelter and make copies of it to distribute to checkpoints in the manhunt for the lovers.

The shelter workers sat with her in those first days, trying to calm her down. "You are a brave girl, stop crying," they would say. "You are the one who had the nerve to fight for your rights."

"I feel pity for my parents," Zakia replied. "I miss them, but I am worried about what they will do."

Najeeba had seen this many times before. "In Afghan society families disown their children and do not forgive them," she said. "Thinking about such things would disturb her and make her cry."

"I love him, and I'm not going to give him up," she declared in one breath and then, in the next, "I don't know what to do. On the one hand, there is my lover and on the other hand my family."

She appealed to Najeeba for guidance, but all the other woman could do was tell the girl to look in her own heart. "We would not tell her which side to take," Najeeba said. "It is her decision. But we always said, 'Think carefully before you make any decision.'"

Zakia always came back to the same thing. "I want to marry the boy."

"If that is what you really want, then do it," Najeeba said.

"Don't you think it is wrong?"

"Whatever your heart believes cannot be wrong," Najeeba said. "Now that you have fallen in love, you should fight for it till the end, until you achieve what you have wished for. Once you are married, you can still try to reconcile with your family. It might take a few years, four or five or even eight years. It might happen soon, or it might take a while."

The easiest way to calm her crying fits was to get her talking about Ali.

"Tell us what his good qualities are. What qualities made you want to marry him?" Najeeba would say.

"He is supportive, and when you have the support of someone, that's everything you can expect in your life. You always seek someone who will stand by your side and support you all the time, and he has all these good qualities. He is very kind, active, and he belongs to a very gentle family," she would reply. "I have so much love for him, and I feel that he loves me as much as I love him. He is hardworking, and he is ready to sacrifice everything for me," Zakia said.

"Besides," she would add with a smile, "he is handsome."

When she was calmer, she mixed well with the other girls and young women, many of them about her age. She had a keen sense of her rights as a person and lectured the other girls on that. By all accounts the prettiest of Zaman's seven daughters, Zakia grew up adored by her father and either admired or envied by her siblings, which gave her a self-possession unusual in a young Afghan woman, a self-possession that had turned to anger and resentment when her brothers tried to control her once she came of age. "Although she was uneducated, she kept everyone busy. She used to make jokes, tell stories, recite poetry," Najeeba said. "She had a very funny and charming personality, and once Zakia was in the shelter, all of the girls were actively involved with her. She was a good, active, brave, amusing girl."

As weeks turned to months, though, she grew disenchanted. "At first I was happy at the shelter," Zakia said. "Later on I realized they couldn't resolve my case." She began to ask for permission to leave the shelter so she could be with Ali. Technically, women's shelters are not jails, but in practice they function that way by agreement between the courts and the police, women's groups, and the women themselves. Shelter officials repeatedly convened a committee of representatives from these groups to discuss whether Zakia could be safely discharged, as she requested.

"The committee members said, 'If we allow her to leave, where would she go?'" Najeeba said. One or another of Zakia's family members were always waiting outside the shelter or, if they went to court, outside that building. The committee repeatedly turned down her request.

Such groups are one of the laudable outcomes of Afghanistan's landmark Elimination of Violence Against Women (EVAW) law—but as Zakia found, they are also examples of its limitations. When the EVAW law was enacted in 2009, it was hailed as a model of legislation on behalf of oppressed women in many underdeveloped countries. At first glance the Afghan constitution adopted after the fall of the Taliban had already admirably enshrined the rights of women.[1] Written with expert help from American and European scholars, it declared that women should have equal rights with men, that a girl became a legal adult with full civil rights at age eighteen, that no girl could be married before the age of sixteen and would have to consent to any marriage, and so forth. The problem was, there were no penalties decreed for violating those declarations of equality and no enabling legislation was enacted to, for instance, penalize a father who married his daughter off at age fourteen or beat his wife because she glanced at another man. Under the Afghan penal code, even rape was not a crime—unmentioned in civil and criminal law, it was treated as a family matter, under the purview of shariah law religious courts. Similarly, shariah law was all that applied if a husband beat his wife, even if he beat her to death; more often than not, the shariah court would approve of his crime if it was based on his belief that some transgression of his patriarchal rights had taken place.

The EVAW law changed that. Rape, wife beating, and forced and child marriage were given criminal penalties. Many customary practices were outlawed; one of those was what the EVAW law called "denial of relationship," the practice of families controlling a person's choice of spouse. Prior to EVAW, Zakia in effect had no legal right to choose to marry Ali; that choice belonged to her father alone, no matter her age. Prior to EVAW, the lovers would have been jailed and prosecuted for attempted adultery at the least, and adultery if there was a suspicion of sexual relations. Adultery was subject to penalties ranging from flogging to ten years in jail, or even to death by stoning.[2] Without EVAW women's shelters would not have the role they've come to have, in protecting women from violence that had not even been a crime prior to the passing of the law, and without shelters like the one in Bamiyan, Zakia would have long since perished. If there is one thing more than any other that made the story of Zakia and Ali possible, it was the EVAW law. In a way they had the Taliban to thank for it. The suppression of women during their six years in power had outraged most of the world, and after their fall the promotion of decent treatment for Afghan women was a cornerstone of international policy toward Afghanistan. EVAW was a direct outcome of Western intervention and a response to the excesses of the Taliban regime that preceded it.

Nonetheless, Zakia and Ali were lucky to have survived for as long as they had. EVAW is also an imperfect law, particularly when it comes to implementation in a fiercely patriarchal society and in backward, rural places where most judges have no law degree or any other legal qualification; many still believe that the world is flat and that it is nonsense or blasphemy to suggest otherwise.

In another Hazara community a year and a half before, in Ghazni Province, a sixteen-year-old girl named Sabira was lashed a hundred and one times after being accused of adultery—although she later was proven to still be a virgin. Her only crime was to have been alone in a shop with a man she said had raped her. She was apparently too inexperienced to understand what constituted rape.[3] EVAW law meant nothing in her defense, local judges refused to apply it, and the mullahs and former jihadi commanders who ordered the lashing were never punished, even after a nationwide outcry.

As long as there were no judges in Bamiyan willing to sanction Zakia's family for staking out the Bamiyan shelter and the courts, implicitly but clearly threatening violence against her if she got out, the limitation of EVAW law there was just as clear. Only the intervention of people like Fatima Kazimi, the head of the women's ministry in Bamiyan, and shelter officials protected her from her family's retribution.

Despite the threat they posed to her, Zakia's own family members had visiting privileges, and her mother and father came frequently, as did her sisters. "They would urge me to come home and would say, 'This is not good, this is not fair that you are here,'" Zakia said. "They would not curse me, just try to make me understand. They would tell me, 'Don't be afraid of us. We're not going to do anything to you.' But I knew they couldn't force me to come home with them, so this was the way to get me to come home, and I knew what they would do to me. One hundred percent, they would kill me even before they got me home. Before coming to the shelter, just for having an affair they were threatening and beating me. Now that I had done this big thing by running away, I knew they would do something terrible to me," she said.

Zakia's case went to court several times, where the judges, who were all Tajiks like Zakia's family, would insist that she could marry Ali only with her father's consent. Ali's family claimed that Zaman and his sons had bribed the judges to side with them, and

Zaman claimed that Anwar and his sons had bribed the women's ministry, the police, and the governor's office to support Zakia. Possibly all of them were right; corruption is pervasive in Afghanistan, particularly in Bamiyan. Still, both sides would have been taking bribes to act in line with their ethnic allegiances.

Like most Afghan judges, the chief judge of the Bamiyan Province Primary Court, Judge Attaullah Tamkeen, was not a law-school graduate.[4] His only legal experience was the study of shariah law at Balkh University, according to one of his legal colleagues on the panel that heard Zakia's case, Judge Saif Rahman, who also had no law degree. Some Afghan judges are even less educated, being only graduates of madrassas, religious schools where the students spend most of their time learning to recite the entire Koran from memory. In a society that reveres its male elders, most judges are old, and whatever legal knowledge they have predates Afghanistan's current constitution and any legislation of the last decade that gave women some rights, in particular the EVAW law. If the judges had a passing acquaintance with Afghanistan's constitution, they would know that Zakia was legally an adult and entitled to choose her own spouse. EVAW law makes her rights more explicit and criminalizes her family's acts, although "denial of relationship" is probably the least prosecuted of all crimes in Afghanistan.

"In any society it's not just the law that shapes everything," said Rubina Hamdard, a lawyer with the Afghan Women's Network who followed this case closely. "It's the behavior of the judges and how they implement the law. Here in Afghanistan and in this case especially, it's true, judges are the limitation of the law. Judges resolve runaway cases by sentencing the girls to one year in jail even though they're over eighteen and although there isn't a law against running away—but there is a law against penalizing running away."

Backed up by the Bamiyan court, her family's persistence finally wore Zakia down, and on February 2, 2014, she was taken out of the shelter to meet her mother, her father, and three of the judges, along with half a dozen elders from their village. Their version is that she had petitioned to be released to them; her version is that she had petitioned to be released on her own because she was eighteen. At the hearing, Judge Tamkeen had called in her family members and worked out an agreement. They pledged not to kill or otherwise harm her for having run away from home, and they would drop any charges against her (this court was still treating running away as if it were a crime). Her father, her uncle, and several elders all put their thumbprints on a document approved by Judge Tamkeen, confirming the agreement to take her home from the shelter and not to harm her, and her consent to that. Called before Judge Tamkeen, surrounded by her obviously angry relatives, Zakia agreed.

Pledges like the one signed by Zakia's family have dubious value. For all the talk about Afghan honor, the concept of honor as it is applied in Afghanistan has nothing to do with keeping one's word, especially when it comes to promising not to kill a woman.

Gul Meena was an eighteen-year-old who had been married off as a prepubescent child to an abusive husband. She ran away with a neighbor, who became her lover, a man named Qari Zakir, fleeing their village in Kunar Province, in 2012; they managed to marry on the grounds that her previous marriage was illegal. Somehow her brother and father found her a year later and visited on the pretense of reconciling with her.[5] When they left, Mr. Zakir lay dead in his bed, his head nearly severed from his neck with a knife. Ms. Meena lay grievously wounded in the next bed, her head mangled by fifteen blows from an ax; police were seeking the brother for personally carrying out the attack. Such ultraviolence is often a distinguishing characteristic of honor killings[6] in Afghanistan. They are rarely "clean" kills, and instead reveal the depth of hatred and passion aroused by the woman's transgression. By some miracle and thanks to the work of the doctors at the hospital in Jalalabad, Gul Meena managed to survive; sympathetic journalists and aid workers donated money to help finance her care and pay for medication and food,[7] since she had no family left that would do so.

It is common for families to resort to subterfuge to get runaway women back. In a village in Dashte Archi District in Kunduz, in 2010, a twenty-five-year-old man named Khayyam and a nineteen-year-old woman named Siddiqa wanted to marry, but the woman's family had already promised her to someone else. The couple fled to Kunar Province, but emissaries from both families came to them to persuade them that all was forgiven and they could return to their village to be married properly. Instead, when they got there, the entire male population of the village turned out to watch the local Taliban commander pronounce them guilty of adultery and sentence them to death by stoning. They were both put in separate large holes while their neighbors and family members began chucking stones at them. Interviewed later, Nadir Khan, one of the villagers, did not object to the stoning, though he said that he did not himself throw stones. As it began, "They said, 'We love each other no matter what happens,'" he related.[8] The stoning was enthusiastic, and some of the villagers picked up rocks so heavy they were hard to lift, pummeling the couple from close range. The evidence of the crowd's enthusiasm for the executions was clear from video recordings made on several villagers' cell phones, copies of which began circulating nationally on social-media sites.[9] Siddiqa was seen sinking slowly to her knees and then, after being hit on the head by one especially large stone, collapsing to the bottom of the pit they had put her in, apparently unconscious; her agony was obscured from view by the blue burqa she wore. When she recovered and tried to crawl out of the pit, one of the men shot her three times in the head with his AK-47. Her lover, Khayyam, could not be seen in the video, as so many of his neighbors were crowded so closely around him; he was stoned to death in minutes.[10] Although the stonings were carried out by the Taliban, after the village later fell into government hands, the Afghan police were reluctant to prosecute most of the perpetrators, despite abundant video evidence of their apparently willing involvement in the crime.[11]

Like any young woman in Afghan society, Zakia well knew what awaited her if she went astray, but it was also hard for her to believe that those closest to her could become her killers, and she said that she vacillated from wanting desperately to believe their assurances to knowing she was lost if she did. "They pressured me to make me say that I wanted to go with my parents. I had to say that. I had no way to say no," Zakia said.

Judge Tamkeen took her aside and gave her a lecture about ethnic loyalty. "Do not marry that boy, or you will dishonor me and our entire ethnic group," Judge Tamkeen said, according to Zakia's account. Like most of the judges in Bamiyan, he was Tajik and a Sunni Muslim. Ali as well as Fatima Kazimi, the head of the women's ministry in Bamiyan, and most of the other officials in Bamiyan including police were all Hazaras and Shia Muslims.

None of the representatives from the women's shelter were present during that hearing—Najeeba Ahmadi, the shelter head, had gone to Kabul on personal business and returned only toward the end of the day, and Fatima Kazimi had not been informed of it. Late in the day, after hours of pressure by the crowd of officials and family, Zakia agreed to put her thumbprint on the document consenting to her return to her family. Najeeba had arrived by then and was told of the agreement; she stalled for time, saying it was too late in the day, there was paperwork to do before she could legally release Zakia, and they should all come back in the morning. She spent the night working the phones, alerting other women's leaders and sympathetic officials to what was about to happen.

The next morning, February 3, Najeeba brought Zakia from the shelter to the court, where her family had assembled again; this time the group was larger, including her brother Gula Khan, two male cousins, her parents, Sabza and Zaman, the six village elders, plus the panel of three judges, headed by Judge Tamkeen. Fatima Kazimi was also there, backed up by the deputy governor, Asif Mubaligh, and the deputy police chief, Ali Lagzi.

Fatima Kazimi is a presence; big and slightly rotund, usually dressed in a purple silk head scarf and a dark modesty trench coat, she exudes self-assurance and authority. Fatima and the deputy governor took Zakia aside, over the strenuous objections of her family. "Do you understand," Fatima asked her, "that you have signed an agreement to return home with your family?"

"Yes," Zakia said in a small voice.

"You don't have to do it," Fatima said. "You can always change your mind, and we will protect you if you do. You just have to say in court, in front of the judges, that you don't want to go."

When they returned to the courtroom, Zakia stood up and said she wanted to stay in the shelter. Judge Tamkeen leaped to his feet and ordered policemen to take her out by force and return her to the family. Zakia screamed, "I don't want to go home!"

The judge threatened to send them all to jail.

"This is a violence against her and a violence against women," Fatima retorted. "You can't do this." She asked the deputy police chief to intervene, and he ordered the policemen to bring Zakia back to the shelter; in the end the policemen obeyed their superiors, who were fellow Hazaras, and not the judges, who were Tajiks.

Zakia's family then dropped all pretenses of not wishing her harm. Her father and brother tried to drag her physically away from Fatima and the police, but her mother was the worst of them.

"You whore!" Sabza screamed at her, about the worst thing any Afghan mother—or any mother—could say to her daughter.

One of the men yelled, "You will not live in peace! We will kill you!"

"My mother was shouting and cursing me, my brothers and my aunt's son tried to beat me, my father and mother were tearing at my clothes and even pulling my clothes off," Zakia said. "I felt that if they got me out of there, I wouldn't have gotten home. They would have killed me on the way."

"They were ferocious," Fatima said. "There was no question in our mind—of course she would be killed if they ever got their hands on her."

The girl's scarf was ripped from her head, and Sabza pulled her jacket off as the family struggled with police to get her back.

"This girl must be hanged!" shouted Zaman.

"That was their plan. That was their decision," Zakia said. "At least then the police also found out that they would kill me, so they assured me they would not hand me over."

Zaman and his son were handcuffed and arrested and held until

they calmed down, while the police pushed Sabza out of the courtroom, still screaming and cursing.

The deputy governor and the deputy police chief, as well as Najeeba Ahmadi, Fatima Kazimi, and the head of the human-rights
office, Aziza Ahmadi, all witnessed the outburst and her family's
passionate vows to kill Zakia. These could have been dismissed as
being said in the heat of the moment, the sort of harsh words uttered in a family conflict that go far beyond any settled intention,
except that their anger did not dissipate. Weeks and months later,
Najeeba was still receiving telephoned death threats from Zakia's
family, and they would eventually give up their farm, their liveli-
hood, and their home in the single-minded pursuit of vengeance
against Zakia and Ali.

After the Bamiyan courtroom melee, a furious Judge Tamkeen
issued an order suspending Fatima Kazimi and Aziza Ahmadi from
their jobs. He even ordered Fatima's arrest for questioning by the
attorney general's office. "The attorney general asked us to bring
her in for interrogation," said Bamiyan provincial police chief
General Khudayar Qudsi. "But there is no basis for such action,
so we will not recognize such requests." The governor simply told
police to ignore the order, and Fatima continued to go to work.[12]

Zakia was safe back in the shelter, but her problem was no
closer to being solved. Fatima acceded to Ali's request to be allowed to visit Zakia at the shelter, something normally *not* allowed,
and Fatima claimed later she knew he would smuggle in a telephone but looked the other way when he did. By then Zakia and
Ali were both experts in clandestine calling, and they began plot-
ting her escape.

There was no longer any reason to stay in the shelter; as far as
the lovers could see, it offered no solutions, only a temporary safety
that could end anytime without warning. The judges and Zakia's
family had the weight of Afghan social custom and practice on
their side and the potential authority of the central government
behind them. Even many of Ali's fellow Hazaras disapproved of
the couple's actions.

They were also well aware of the many examples of the fate

awaiting an Afghan woman who goes astray and is returned to an angry family. "One hundred percent, they would kill me," Zakia had said—and who could know her own family better than one of its daughters? Had Fatima not intervened to prevent Zakia from going back home with her family, she might have ended up like Amina, a teenage girl from northern Baghlan Province, who was either fifteen or eighteen years old.[13] The daughter of a man named Khuda Bakhsh, Amina fled from her family's home when her father proposed to marry her to a much older man in their village in Tala Wa Barfak District.[14] Police found her wandering in the bazaar in the provincial capital of Pul-e-Kumri, asking people how to find the women's-ministry offices. She was arrested, essentially, for being a woman alone.

The police bypassed the jail and took her directly to the provincial women's ministry, on March 20, 2014—the day before Zakia escaped her shelter, in fact—and handed her over to Uranus Atifi, head of the legal department; she was put in a shelter in Pul-e-Kumri and stayed there for the following month. Then a member of the provincial council, Samay Faisal, called Ms. Atifi and said that Amina's brother and uncle had come to Pul-e-Kumri and wanted to take the girl home. Mr. Faisal offered to vouch for them, she said, so she brought the family in, and they all signed guarantee papers promising not to harm the girl if she came home and not to force her to marry the fiancé she had rejected.

"Before handing her over to her family, we talked to Amina in private and asked her if she wanted to go back to her home," Ms. Atifi said. "She said that she did want to go back, because she didn't want her case to get bigger and create more problems." Ms. Atifi took the precaution of videoing the family's pledges not to hurt the girl and the girl's consent to return. Still, Ms. Atifi was worried, and she got the brother's phone number and called him to speak to Amina while they were driving back.

"That same night I called her at eight P.M., and I talked to her and asked her if she was all right. She told me she was and that they were still driving. At ten P.M. I called them again, but this time I couldn't get through," Ms. Atifi said.

The next morning Ms. Atifi called the brother, and he coolly related to her that a group of nine armed men wearing masks had stopped their car and dragged Amina out and shot her to death but harmed no one else. The family had not bothered to report the crime to the police. The brother seemed to her suspiciously calm about his sister's murder.

No one believed the family's story that the masked men must have been relatives of the jilted fiancé. If that were the case, skeptics asked, why wouldn't the outraged fiancé's relatives have killed the brother, uncle, and cousin who were there, too, and who were supposedly returning the girl to her home and canceling her engagement?

"You know, if a husband sees his wife in bed with a stranger and kills her, he gets one year in prison at most," said Shahla Farid, a female professor of law who is on the board of the Afghan Women's Network. "If she kills her husband for the same thing, she can be executed. That's right there in the Afghan penal code."[15] More likely the husband would not be prosecuted in such a case or, if prosecuted, get anything more than a toke punishment.[16]

"I believe the two families reached an agreement, but I'm not sure," said Khadija Yaqeen, the director of women's affairs in Baghlan Province. "We don't care what deal or interfamily agreement is made or will be made. Someone was killed, and there has to be an investigation so that justice is done in Amina's case." As in so many similar ones, that apparently never happened.[17]


In Bamiyan nearly two months went by after the court hearing. In the end Zakia's father forced matters to a head by formally requesting that the court in Bamiyan transfer Zakia's case to Kabul. There, he thought, he would get a better reception, since police and government officials in the capital would not be Hazaras but Tajiks or Pashtuns, and if a judge ordered her returned to the family, the police would obey. "We talked with the girl and got her consent to transfer her case to Kabul," said Zaman. Zakia of course said she gave no such consent and that the impending transfer precipitated her decision to escape, which she did the night before it was scheduled.

Coming so soon before the transfer, the elopement, Zaman felt, had to have been staged by women's-ministry officials. "We were not even allowed to meet her in person, so we talked to her on the phone and got her consent," Zaman said. "She agreed to come home. She is not guilty at all. It is the women's director, who thought she might be in trouble due to her involvement in the case, who decided to help them escape. Otherwise how can a girl from a shelter which is guarded by police[18] escape? It must be direct involvement of that woman and others who arranged her escape." Fatima Kazimi and Najeeba Ahmadi denied Zaman's claims, as did Ali and Zakia later on.

Unknown to them all, however, Zaman's appeals to move the case to Kabul had nothing to do with the impending transfer. Shukria Khaliqi, who was then a lawyer with the group Women for Afghan Women (WAW), had heard about the case and formally requested that it be moved to the capital, with the approval of women's-ministry officials in Kabul and women's advocates in the attorney general's office. In Kabul they thought they could find a court with judges who were lawyers and who had a passing acquaintance with the law. Shukria was convinced she could win the case for the couple. Then, although they would still be at risk of attack from Zakia's family, there would be no legal impediment to their marriage and no justification for keeping Zakia in a shelter.

Before WAW could reach Zakia to tell her all this, however, the couple was already on the run. Zakia's father pressed kidnapping charges against Ali, so they were fugitives not only from her family's retribution but from the law as well. They were together, but as far as the Afghan police were concerned—and that included the police in Bamiyan—they were wanted criminals who needed to be hunted down. Fellow feeling among Hazaras goes only so far; a woman on the run would always be in the wrong in the view of Afghan authority of whatever ethnic background.

Once Zakia and Ali had escaped, however, they also became heroes to many Afghans, especially to women and young people.

Najeeba Ahmadi of the Bamiyan shelter, while insisting she had no role in Zakia's escape, nonetheless applauded her at the time it happened. "Her action shows that everyone has the right to marry according to their own will. She has tried to achieve her own wishes. Her resistance and bravery are a good example for all those women and girls who want to protect their rights. When women resist for their rights, they have the ability to achieve their goals. I don't believe Zakia has done anything wrong. Her actions are admirable, and wherever she is, I wish her the best of luck and success in her life."

Zakia and Ali themselves had modest goals. They knew that most couples who eloped were usually caught, with terrible consequences. They never expected to get very far but were determined to have some real time together while they could, even if it meant death for both of them.

4

# A RABBI AMONG THE MULLAHS

The e-mail from Rabbi Shmuley Boteach on March 25, 2014, was enigmatic and urgent. "I just heard very important info about the case. Can we speak please?" Shmuley was among hundreds of readers who had gotten in touch with me after I wrote about the plight of Zakia and Ali in the *New York Times*. At the time of that first article,[1] Zakia was on month four or five of her stay at the Bamiyan Women's Shelter, her disastrous court hearing was behind her, and Ali was mooning around the valley, trying to figure out an escape plan.

Many of those readers wanted to help the couple; Rabbi Shmuley was just a bit more pushy than most, and he now had the personal e-mail address and phone number I had given him, so he was not about to let up. Somewhat wearily I called him back, because I knew he wouldn't rest until I had. Part of me had given up on Zakia and Ali after I wrote that first story; I just didn't see how their story could end well, unless the then-president, Hamid Karzai, decided to step in and resolve it for them by decree. He was quite capable of doing this had he been interested, but in this case any interest he had was bound to be negative. The earnest and well-meaning efforts of a rabbi from New Jersey were not going to sway the president of the Islamic Republic of Afghanistan, a country where most other faiths are forbidden, the only consecrated Christian church is a small chapel inside the Italian embassy, and the lone synagogue has but one surviving congregant. Plus, at that time in his administration President Karzai was scarcely on speaking terms with American officials, despite his country's dependence on American aid.[2] So, not expecting much, I called Shmuley's number in North Jersey from our bureau in Kabul.

Shmuley's assistant put me straight through, and the rabbi got right to the point, addressing me, as he always had in our many previous calls, as if we were old friends. "Rod, she escaped."

"Who?"

"Zina, Zophia, what was her name?"

"Zakia?"

"Yes, she escaped, a couple nights ago. I just heard about it."

"Who from?"

"Fatima told me."

"Really?"

I didn't know that Fatima Kazimi, the women's director from Bamiyan, was in touch with Rabbi Shmuley; he was full of surprises and, as I would see, quite determined. Fatima was the reason I knew about Zakia and Ali—and by many accounts, in particular her own, the only reason Zakia was not already dead.

The whole affair of Zakia and Ali had come to my attention only a couple of months earlier, when, on February 9, Fatima Kazimi had e-mailed every journalist working in Afghanistan for major American publications. She dictated the e-mail through her English-speaking son and sent it to me by clicking on my byline on NYTimes.com:

Dear Mr. Nordland:[3]

I'm Fatima Kazimi, Bamyan Director of Department of Women's Affairs (DoWA), the provincial branch of Ministry of Women's Affairs (MoWA.) We are the lead protector/defender of women's rights in Bamyan province, Afghanistan.

I just go straightly to the point which is the case of a girl

(Tajik ethnicity) and a boy (Hazara ethnicity) that fled from their houses and came to Bamyan Department of Women's Rights (DoWA) and Bamyan Independent Human Rights Commission for the sake of safety, protection and to finally make their dream a reality, marriage. We follow up this case from its inception about three months ago, and videotaped the confession and speeches of the lovers.

As the marriage of different ethnicity in Afghanistan and especially in Bamyan is counted as a taboo, the girl's family insisting in their daughter's return as well as so many other hands that get involved in this case.

As the girl doesn't want to return to her family, and the fact that it is involved a high risk of girl's murder if she gets back (as we saw in previous cases), the DoWA and other women's rights protector including the Governor Office, Independent Human Rights Commission and Civil Society Forum continues their advocacy for this lovers.

However, instead of supporting and protecting women's rights in Bamyan, the Provincial Court has ordered my suspension and two others from our job and prosecution just because we are following this case so closely and the FACT THAT MOST OF THE JUDGES in provincial court are from Tajik ethnicity.

You can contact Bamyan Governor Office, and the Independent Human Rights Commission to verify this information and plenty of other information that we have. I was wondering if you broadcast this news as you will protect the life of this couple and the fact that we are being threatened to death.

I'm looking forward to hearing from you,
Best regards.
Fatima Kazimi

I called her right away and asked a few exploratory questions—chiefly, would the couple talk and could we take pictures? Fatima said yes and maybe. That was good enough for me. We were on the next flight to Bamiyan, aboard East Horizon Airlines, which flies to Bamiyan, sometimes twice weekly, sometimes not for months on end. I took with me photojournalist Mauricio Lima and our Afghan colleague Jawad Sukhanyar. A year or two earlier, we could have driven the six to eight hours over one of the two passes through the Hindu Kush into Bamiyan, but both have now been effectively cut off, at least for foreigners, by intermittent Taliban ambushes.

I was already primed to jump on such a story and had long been looking for this sort of opportunity. Honor killings are more often than not one of Afghanistan's dirty little secrets; instances where they come into the open are rare, and it is even more rare to have a chance to write about stopping a threatened honor killing, especially when the parties were willing to talk and perhaps even be photographed. We were en route before Fatima had a chance to change her mind; I didn't even call her again, for fear she would reconsider, and the next time she heard from us, we were knocking on her office door in the Bamiyan government office building not far from the airstrip.

Fatima received us from behind an expansive glass-topped desk, framed by windows and the glare from sunlit snow, in a room with walls lined with chairs for supplicants. After summarizing what had happened to Zakia and Ali, Fatima went to fetch Zakia from the women's shelter, bringing her back to the office under a heavy guard, two green Ford Ranger pickup trucks full of policemen. Zakia had her shawl on but was dressed in loud, bright colors, as I would come to learn she usually was, a pink head scarf and an orange sweater. She caused a stir among the policemen and the government officials who lined the hallways as she was brought in; Afghans find her beautiful, with startlingly large, amber eyes.

She was tongue-tied at first. It was not only the first time she'd ever seen a journalist, it was the first time she'd ever seen a foreigner and the first time in her life that she'd ever talked to a male stranger—moreover, the first time she'd ever talked to a man other than Ali, and Anwar, and her brothers and father. "I knew, because of my case, I had to have that courage to speak. I realized that," she said much later, recalling how terrified she'd been that day.

Expressing herself seemed painful, but with Fatima gently nudging her along, her story poured out through Jawad, who translated. "My whole family is against my marriage," she said. "I want to go ahead anyway. I request of you, I don't want to stay in Bamiyan. I can live anywhere but in Bamiyan. All I want is my love.

"The judges told me, 'We are Tajik and it's dishonoring us if you decide to marry a Hazara.' The judges, my mother, and father were all saying this to me, but I told them whatever he might be, he's still a Muslim. I'm very worried about him and his safety. My father and relations threatened him, and I'm afraid they might do something. I get death threats from my family. They say if I go marry him, they will not let us live, and if I go home, my mother and father will not let me live."

Even her sister turned against her, she said. During a visit with her at the shelter, "she started screaming at me, using abusive words. You could hear her all over the building."

Zakia continued, "I love him, and now even if I don't get to marry him, I couldn't live here, I can't go back and stay here, I have to leave forever. I have confidence in him. I know his attitudes and his good moral character. I want to live with him."

In the court proceeding, Zaman could not argue that his daughter had run away or chosen an improper mate, since neither of those acts is a crime. But breaking an engagement *is* a matter for the Afghan courts, and so her father began his suit by claiming that she had been formally engaged to her nephew, which Zakia said was the first she had heard of it.

"They kept getting it mixed up, though," Fatima said with a laugh. "One minute they claimed she was engaged to her father's sister's son, the next it was her mother's sister's son. They should make up their minds before lying like that."

Zakia's account came out fitfully and slowly at first, with long, awkward silences and monosyllabic replies. The most extraordinary thing about her was the way her rare smile could suddenly illuminate her face, enlivening everything—eyes, lips, nose. It would flicker on like sunlight from a gap in a fast-moving cloud and be just as quickly gone. Her smile would transform her so thoroughly and so engagingly that you wanted to find some way to summon it back again.

I explained to her the probable consequences of an article quoting her openly. People in Bamiyan would see it through local Internet connections, however rickety. All news is global, especially if it appears in the *New York Times*. Local news organizations might well pick it up, too. Everything she said to us would likely be heard or read by everyone she knows; if her relatives could not read, someone who *could* read would relate it to them.

Zakia's only response was that she had already been in the shelter in Bamiyan for nearly five months. She had a point. In all that time, the closest she came to resolving her status had been the abortive February 3 court hearing.

At Fatima's suggestion we talked a bit about the shelter and the other girls and young women who were there. Some had been there for years already, unable to get legal resolution such as protection from an abusive spouse and unable to leave for fear of the vengeance of their menfolk—often on both sides of their families. The worst case at the shelter at the time was that of the fourteen-year-old girl Safoora, the Hazara girl who would later help Zakia escape from the shelter. Waylaid in the shabby Bamiyan courthouse while her family disputed details of their daughter's arranged marriage, Safoora was taken into a supply room and gang-raped by four Tajik courthouse employees. The police, Hazaras, arrested the culprits; the Tajik judges vacated the cases against all but one of them—and then charged him with adultery, a criminal offense in Afghanistan, rather than rape. Then the judges lodged a similar charge of adultery against Safoora. It was absurd, because even in Afghanistan a child can never give legal consent, even if the sex had been on some physical level "consensual"—however implausible that would be in a courthouse gang rape. While the women's advocates tried to get the criminal charges against her dismissed, Safoora was kept in the shelter—primarily to ensure that her family did not honor-kill her to erase their shame.

Fatima returned to Zakia's predicament, her point clear. "What do you think I should do?" Zakia asked her.

"You have to decide that for yourself." Fatima seemed the concerned, kindly auntie.

"Will it help us reach each other?" Zakia asked me.

"Possibly," I said, not convinced. "Possibly someone like your president would read about what happened and intervene, but honestly, probably not. On the other hand, what alternatives do you have now?"

This was a girl who had never been to school, who could neither read nor write, and whose knowledge of alphanumeric characters extended to just ten digits, 1 through 0 on the telephone keypad. Only one of the eleven children in Zakia's family, nine-year-old Razak, had ever been to school. Zakia sat with her back straight against the wall, her nose still bruised from the courtroom tussle. Her colorful layers of artificial silks, tunics, and pantaloons, in the brilliance of the glare, seemed cheap and tawdry when looked at individually, little holes and rips and tears showing here and there, but their overall effect was to enhance her attractiveness. She stared at the floor for most of our conversation, and I felt that she must be wondering, "Why are these foreigners interested in me?"

She thought about it for a spell. Then she raised her head and for the first time looked me right in the eye and said, "I don't mind," and smiled briefly.

Mauricio, the photographer, had been dozing, as photographers often do during interviews when there's nothing to shoot; now it was his turn to ask for permission to photograph her. This was even touchier than the interview. Photography of Afghan women is widely forbidden, notwithstanding some famous images—the iconic green-eyed refugee girl, Sharbat Gula, photographed by Steve McCurry for *National Geographic*,[4] for instance. Because Sharbat was a child, just twelve years old at the time, it was allowed, as it would have been for older women, usually widowed and desperate and therefore excused from the strictures that normally apply. Otherwise even shooting a woman in a head-to-toe burqa can provoke men in the vicinity, whether they're related to the woman or not, to attack a photographer. Asked for permission to be photographed, most young women in Afghanistan will understandably say no.[5]

This time, however, Zakia did not think about it long at all. "I don't mind," she said, and Mauricio got right to work. The mysteries of the camera's unblinking eye; I had fully expected that Mauricio would be returning to Kabul disappointed. Every interaction between photographer and subject is a kind of seduction, in one direction or the other, and that was true even between Zakia and Mauricio, a talented photographer who looks more like a nightclub bouncer and who firmly believes in the dictum that the best picture is taken up close. In this case he got six inches or so from her face, in an effort to compensate for the bright sunlight; he is a master of the awkward portrait. Zakia accepted it with equanimity; after a while she even seemed in some odd way empowered by the attention. She was a beautiful woman who it is safe to say had never been properly, if ever, photographed.[6] Here she was being shot by a pro, and she seemed to like it.

It was true that she had little to lose. Earlier she had talked about how large and close the members of her extended family were; in addition to her four brothers, there were many cousins, who in Afghanistan are often as close as siblings. In all, her family's tribe had thirty-five homes in the area. They would all be after Ali now, since they could not get to her in the shelter. "I would wait until I reach my love, no matter how long. But I'm very worried that my family is trying to harm his family, and I'm very worried about that. If he should die, I should also die."

"Are you sure about that?" Fatima cut in and asked her, a little startled by her declaration.

Zakia looked straight at her. "Of course."

Fatima frowned. She might have approved of romantic love, or at least the legal right to pursue it, but she had a low opinion of men, honed no doubt during two years of advocating in cases of violence against women brought under the EVAW law, and she didn't think any of them were worth dying for. She reminded Mauricio to take her own picture as well, which he dutifully did.

"This is my story, too," she said. "Don't forget that you have to write about me." She looked at me sternly; I made no comment.

Later Mauricio took Zakia and Fatima outside. As Fatima and

Zakia crossed the street, Mauricio crouching and shooting, their police escort went wild and began screaming and cursing at him. One policeman unshouldered his automatic rifle and aimed it at him. They did not think it right to photograph women, whether the women had agreed to it or not. After all, how can a woman possibly give consent without a man to speak for her?

To the policemen and many others in Afghan society, this encounter would likely encapsulate the disconnect between Afghan and Western culture. It meant something else altogether to Zakia.

"It gave me hope," she said. "I was happy, because now I knew there were people who wanted to help us and cared about us." The outside world might have been mysterious to both Zakia and Ali, but they felt it was something important, and its interest in them was somehow validating. As they well knew, in the eyes of their own society, in the rules and strictures of their culture, they were now outcasts. That these apparently important foreigners were accepting them on their own terms and seemed to feel that what the lovers wanted was not in the slightest unreasonable—and was even praiseworthy—seemed powerfully enabling to this pair of isolated young people.

We had already reached Ali on his cell phone, but he felt safest meeting us at the women's ministry. Fatima felt it would be best if that meeting did not take place on the same day as Zakia's visit, so her family's spies in the government couldn't claim that Fatima was arranging assignations between them.

Ali came the next day, and it was not surprising that he was a handsome young man and a tad vain about his looks. His lush black hair was swept up and back in a pompadour, his beard close-shaven, his trousers tight, and his artificial saddle-leather shoes both pointy and holey. Like Zakia, he was poor, but he had style. His eyes were an arresting shade of golden amber, and what was most striking—I had to check the pictures of Zakia to be sure—nearly the same rare color as hers. On his cheek was a prominent, deep-set bruise, and I asked about it.

"Since this love story began, I have had two bad accidents," he said.

*Since this love story began.* I would soon learn that Ali often referred to Zakia and himself as the participants in a love story, as
if some higher power had written it for them and they were mere
mortals acting out their roles.

The first accident that he referred to was when the Humvee he
was in while on military duty rolled, three years earlier, and ruined
his leg. The second "accident" was the bruise his brother Ismatullah gave him when Ali tried to get to Zakia as she pleaded for his
father to take her in.

Unlike Zakia, Ali was never surprised that people were interested in their story and what had befallen them. It seemed to him
natural and inevitable. "Our story is the same as Shirin and Farhad," he said. "We are stuck in such a story."

It is an old Persian story, immensely popular in Afghanistan
and retold in many forms in popular culture, but particularly in
folk and pop songs. Shirin, the beautiful princess, tells the stonecutter Farhad that she is promised to the prince but that if he could
move a mountain for her with his pickax, she would marry him
instead. So he sets about carving the face off a nearby mountain,
and when the prince sees he has nearly finished what had seemed
an.impossible task, he sends a witch to whisper to Farhad that Shirin has already married the prince. Despondent, he kills himself,
and when she finds that out, she, too, kills herself.

How is this their story? I asked Ali. "If in this temporary world,
they don't reach each other, then God knows they might be able to
do so in the next world," he explained. Every great love must be
doomed to experience its happy endings in some afterlife, it seems,
whether Romeo and Juliet or Shirin and Farhad? He didn't know
the story of Romeo and Juliet, so we summarized it for him; he
especially liked the ending. "My ambition is also the same. Even if
I were killed with my fiancée, I would have reached my ambition.
If they separated us, I would commit suicide."

A pattern was beginning to emerge in the passions of this shabby,
earnest young man with the shining amber eyes that seemed to
light up when he started telling stories, whether his and her more
recent ones or those ancient tales. When we called him the day

before to arrange meeting him, his ringtone had been a love verse from a song retelling the story of Yousef and Zuleikha. Today's was some lines from an Indian musical about Layla and Majnoon. The Persian poet Nezami's epic retelling of the old Arabian story has circulated in one version or another throughout the subcontinent as well, and it traditionally includes these Arabic verses:

> *I pass through the lands of Layla,*
> *Kissing now this wall, now that wall:*
> *It is not these lands that I love,*
> *But the one who dwells within.*[7]

Ali has of course never read poetry, but his illiteracy has not robbed him of literature, to be sure. It was all there, set to music.

That is how their courtship progressed, in those long, numerous telephone conversations that began when she was still just past childhood and he not yet quite an adult. Over and over they replayed for each other the moment they fell in love, the moment they knew, how they knew. For Ali, what those many months in the army were like and his fear of being rejected because of his deformity (as he imagined it to be). For Zakia, the months during which she wished she had said to him something different from what she had, when he proposed across the wall. When they ran out of gossip about the people they knew, or talk of farm life, or antics of children and animals, he would tell her a story, often one he had told before. Her favorite was Yousef and Zuleikha, the Islamic version of the biblical story of the Prophet Joseph (he of the *Amazing Technicolor Dreamcoat*). In the Islamic telling, Yousef is sold as a slave to Potiphar and falls in love with Potiphar's wife, Zuleikha (who is named only in the Islamic versions, not in the biblical story), but is banished. He finds his love thirty years later, when he has gained freedom, prestige, and power and she has become an old woman but still loves him. One kiss and she is a young beauty again. It is not only a popular story among Afghans and in many Muslim societies, it is also a sacred story, recounted in the Koran approvingly—despite the themes of romantic love triumphing over married rectitude, which are explained theologically as love of a higher sort than the carnal, romantic kind.

"I asked her how she liked it," Ali said. "Her reply to me was that I am ready to wait for you for fifty years."

The first article that I did in the *New York Times* after that trip up to Bamiyan had already generated tremendous interest. But I really began to be deluged with reader mail after I wrote on March 31[8] about Zakia's escape from the shelter and the couple's elopement, with police pursuing them as criminals and Zakia's family after them as well—a story I might have missed if Shmuley hadn't alerted me. Many of those readers demanded that something had to be done to help Zakia and Ali. Not a few readers upbraided me, too: "You've drawn attention to them, now do something about it," one wrote. Little did I appreciate at the time how prophetic those words would become. "Can't the *New York Times* just send a plane in and get them out?" If only it were so simple. None of them were quite as insistent as the rabbi from New Jersey, though, and unlike many of the others, he had a plan, or at least part of a plan. He had a wealthy benefactress, he said, who was determined to spend whatever was required to save the couple's lives, which of course meant getting them to safety somewhere outside Afghanistan. A very wealthy benefactress. Shmuley was not just any rabbi but "America's rabbi," as his own website and some news accounts[9] described him; he was the late singer Michael Jackson's rabbi, he was a television personality, a columnist, a passionate defender of Israel, a self-promoter, a Republican politician, and a friend of Sean Penn and Oprah Winfrey. He runs an organization called the World Values Network,[10] which seeks to promote Jewish values among the wider community, and he has prominent political friends on both sides of the ideological divide in America. He is a consummate networker, a talent he developed during years as Cambridge University's resident rabbi,[11] when he actively invited the interesting and the powerful to speaking and debating engagements and made many lasting friends. He is also an author; his best-known book is *Kosher Sex* and his most recent is *Kosher Lust*.[12] Both are more serious than their titles might suggest and, among other things, promote Shmuley's vision that Jews should make more children—he himself has nine.

Rabbi Shmuley had managed to find Fatima Kazimi's contacts through some social-networking site after he saw her name in the paper, and he'd gotten in touch with her independently. After that first article on Zakia and Ali ran, Fatima was disappointed that the story hadn't focused on her and on her efforts to save the couple, and for a while she'd stopped talking to us. But she was talking to Shmuley, actively. The rabbi had become my back channel to a women's activist in the Hindu Kush, which was only a couple of mountain ranges away from my bureau in Kabul.

The outpouring of interest and offers of help made me feel guilty about the various forces I had unleashed. Would all this publicity really help Zakia and Ali? "You're responsible for them now, I hope you know that," one reader wrote. He had a point. In ways that are hard to fathom, all the publicity had emboldened the couple to make the move they did. Later, when I had occasion to ask Zakia what had given them the courage to flee together, she looked at me with surprise. "Because we knew there were people who cared about us. We knew you would help us." That was an awful leap of faith, but to them it was as if they were no longer alone; if we were interested, so many others would be, and some-how—in ways they had really not thought through very fully—that would solve everything. They were no longer just Zakia and Ali; they were the *story* of Zakia and Ali, which was bigger than they were and as full of promise as it was fraught with danger.

It would not have been the first time that the glare of publicity saved an Afghan woman from an unhappy fate. In 2012 a young woman named Lal Bibi was abducted by a member of an Afghan Local Police (ALP) unit in Kunduz. The ALP are irregular militias that are trained by American Special Forces troops to act as community self-protection. At best they are a well-armed neighborhood watch; at worse they can be a criminal scourge on the communities they're meant to protect. One of the ALP militiamen, who was named Khudaidad, claimed he was entitled to take Lal Bibi in marriage because of an old *baad* contract, an agreement made when she was very young as the result of a dispute between their families. *Baad* is a common practice, in which young girls are exchanged to compensate for a marital infidelity, a murder or other transgression, or just to settle a debt. Lal Bibi and her family claimed there had been no such agreement, and they pressed charges against Khudaidad for raping her and accused three members of his unit, including its commander, of aiding him in her abduction and rape. He calmly defended himself against the charge by claiming he had married her shortly before the rape, and, he told the *New York Times,*[13] "Once the marriage contract is done, any sexual intercourse is not considered rape."

Lal Bibi may have objected to her marriage, but that was forcible marriage, a lesser crime, rather than rape, he said. The policeman produced a mullah who confirmed he had performed the marriage rite before any intercourse took place. The unusual thing about Lal Bibi's case was not so much what had happened to her but that her family members decided to go public about it. After a national outcry, President Hamid Karzai intervened and ordered the ALP unit disbanded. It was but was then quickly replaced with another ALP unit headed by the brother of the commander of the first unit. (Once again a unit allegedly trained and mentored by American special-operations troops). Defying threats and intimidation from the *arbakai* and their friends, Lal Bibi's family traveled to Kabul, where prosecutors eventually sentenced all four police officials involved to sixteen years in prison. During his trial Khudaidad dropped his insistence on the marriage defense and came up with a more novel one. He asked that Lal Bibi's veil be removed during the trial so that, he said, the court could see that she was far too ugly for anyone to have wanted to rape her.[14]

Women's advocates lobbied hard in support of Lal Bibi and her family in that case, and it was a rare win for a female victim of violence.

If Lal Bibi's impoverished and disenfranchised family could prevail against American-backed militiamen, normally accustomed to impunity for their actions, perhaps Zakia and Ali's case was not entirely hopeless. Now that they were free, everything had changed. The sort of money and support that people were offer-ing them could well prove decisive in finding a solution for them, either by paying her family a large enough bride price to go away peaceably or by making it financially plausible for the couple to escape the country. Their story did not have to end there, in some rotting Afghan lockup or at the business end of someone's venge-ful bludgeon. Unfortunately, Zakia and Ali seemed to be well and truly gone. For the moment at least, they had decided that disap-pearing was a safer bet than waiting around for help, even though it meant that no one could find them to offer that help.

❧

# 5

# A BEAUTIFUL PLACE TO HIDE

In plain sight is a good hiding place until it becomes the one place searchers realize they have neglected to look. Zakia and Ali were keenly aware that their time hiding in the house of the village's most prominent citizen was running out. By the end of March, the whole country seemed aroused by the search for the escaped lovers. The Bamiyan police might have been sympathetic to their plight and naturally tended to side with Hazaras, but once Zakia had fled the shelter, she was that most despised of Afghan women, a runaway. The Ministry of Interior in Kabul was leaning on the Bamiyan police to pursue the matter. It was all over Afghan television and radio, on the country's airwaves and news websites—many of which showed no hesitation about lifting and republishing Mauricio Lima's portraits of the lovers from NYTimes.com. The police questioned the Bamiyan shelter's staff and arrested two of its guards, holding them for investigation, although they were ultimately released, since they were guilty of nothing more than falling asleep or not paying enough attention. Fatima Kazimi, the women's-ministry official in Bamiyan, was besieged in her office by Zakia's father and a dozen of his male relatives, who accused her of engineering the escape. Ali's brother Bismillah was arrested and held for four days, his cousin Sattar jailed for two days, and his other brother Ismatullah, himself a police officer, was pressured by his bosses to come clean on his fugitive brother's whereabouts.

Najeeba Ahmadi, the director of the shelter in Bamiyan, felt more than official heat. "I believe that her family would do anything possible against Zakia," Najeeba said. "They even keep calling me using different numbers and threatening me that if they don't get Zakia, they will run me out of Bamiyan or they will kill me to take revenge for Zakia. They don't care how peacefully I try to communicate."

A male voice would come on the line of her personal cell phone. "You've taken our daughter and hidden her somewhere. You know where she is, but you are not telling us. So, for us, you and the girl are the same, and you will both face the consequences."

While all that was going on up in Bamiyan, down in Kabul I was spending an hour every morning wading through reader e-mail, mainly from concerned Americans who assumed I somehow must know how to find the couple and deliver aid to them. Rabbi Shmuley was reenergized to pursue the case. He asked me if I could act as a go-between with the couple, to let them know he had someone standing by ready to rescue them.

"We would like to communicate to them, that we want to help them get out of the country and establish a new life elsewhere where they are not in danger," Shmuley wrote in an e-mail. "But now we have no way of contacting them. If you can assist us with that, I would be very grateful. Please indeed ask them permission, as to whether or not we can be in touch with them."

I was uncomfortable acting as anyone's go-between, but I didn't feel I should just rebuff Shmuley's enthusiastic and heartfelt concern for the couple. My editor in New York, Doug Schorzman, took the matter up with Phil Corbett, the paper's standards editor, and Phil agreed I could introduce Shmuley to an Afghan fixer and translator, so he could have someone who could reach out to Zakia and Ali independently of us. It was also felt that we could share the phone numbers of principals, so long as we had permission from them to do so. Through our Afghan staff, we found a freelance fixer well respected for his integrity, Aimal Yaqubi, who had previously worked for National Public Radio.

That all proved academic, though. Ali was not answering his phone, which was continually giving an "out of coverage area" message, so we couldn't get his permission to give the number to anyone. His father and brothers claimed to have no idea where the two lovers were, other than somewhere in the mountains, and said they too could not reach Ali by telephone. It turned out later that the family had been constrained from saying anything about the couple's whereabouts because Zakia and Ali did not want them to do so.

Zakia's father was on their trail, too. When we interviewed him, it was clear that he had already developed an intimate knowledge about the couple's movements in the days after Zakia's flight from the shelter. He related to us where they had stayed on the first and second nights on the run, the name of the mullah who had attended and tied the *neka* for them, the next place they had stopped farther up the Foladi Valley toward Shah Foladi, and how the police had lost them on the road near the village of Azhdar.

What he didn't suspect, at least not yet, was that they weren't in the mountains any longer but had circled back to Ali's village and were hiding a mere three hundred yards from where Zaman was talking to us at that moment.

"I will not let it go," he said, sitting cross-legged on the floor of his house, his smallest children clustered on either side of him; from oldest to youngest, his brood spanned nearly three decades, with one wife. "I swear to God that even if it costs me everything, I will try to bring my daughter back home. She is a part of my body like one of my limbs—how can I let her go with that boy? Besides that, she was already married, and it is unthinkable to remarry someone else's wife who is already married to someone. It is against every law and shariah. There is no way that I should let her marry that boy."

This accusation of bigamy was a bombshell. Previously Zaman had claimed in court that he had engaged Zakia to his nephew—

and he famously kept changing which aunt had the nephew in question. Now that his daughter had married Ali, he was raising the stakes and claiming that a previous marriage had occurred, that a *neka* had already been tied between Zakia and her first cousin. It is plausible, and even commonplace, for a father to tie a *neka* without his daughter's presence—that is, to marry her to someone formally. All he has to do is swear before a mullah and other witnesses that she has given her consent. Her consent is required, officially, but in practice there is no requirement that such consent needs to be proved, other than by the father's oath. So now to support the bigamy charge, all Zaman would have to do is find a friendly mullah and some like-minded witnesses, then backdate a *neka* document. Even within this new account, he kept muddling his story: At one moment Zakia had run away with the boy; minutes later the boy had kidnapped her. She had escaped from the shelter; Ali had forcibly removed her from it. And so on.

Zaman at first glance did not seem formidable enough to do much of anything. He looked much older than his approximately sixty years, with skin as wrinkled as dried fruit; he was slight and stooped. Five of his eleven children were younger than Zakia, some much younger; the smallest appeared to be not four years old. He was obviously poor, but he also had sons, and cousins, and sons-in-law, and they all crowded into the living room to back him up. "I do not give up easily," he said. "If someone loses his chicken, he will search for it to bring it home. How can I not search for my daughter, who was part of my own liver? I can do everything to get her back. I will try to approach the president, and if that doesn't work, I will decide myself to do something. We are not weak in that sense."

He denied he was threatening any violence—he did not have so much as a nail file to use for a weapon, he said—but the spittle that accompanied his words, the harsh tone, all suggested otherwise, as did the death threats he and his sons had uttered in front of many witnesses in the Bamiyan courthouse. Zaman seemed like nothing so much as a dead daughter's father.

There was no pretense of impotence from Zakia's brother Gula

Khan, who was about twenty or twenty-one. When I reached him by telephone around this time, he screamed at me over the line. His tone told more than his words, which were themselves so blunt and profane they shocked and embarrassed my Afghan colleague Jawad. It was only after I insisted several times that Jawad not hold back that he fully translated Gula Khan's responses to my questions.

"If we were men, we would have done something by now," he said. "If we had cocks, we would take our revenge. How is it possible they steal someone's wife and do not even pay any attention to how we are suffering?

"She really dishonored our family, and the man she was promised to is asking for repayment. He has told us, either find his wife for him and return her or give him ten lakhs of rupees."[1]

"Their whole world was turned upside down when their daughter ran away with a man," said Women for Afghan Women's executive director, Manizha Naderi. Her organization runs seven women's shelters, although not the one in Bamiyan,[2] and Manizha is easily the most effective women's advocate in Afghanistan. "This really shattered their sense of honor within their family and their community. They have no credibility to hold their heads up in front of anyone because of Zakia. And to get their honor back, they think that they have to kill both Ali and especially Zakia. That way they can tell their relatives, 'We are men of honor. We killed her. Our honor is more important than our daughter who has shamed us.' It's really tragic, but most families think this way in Afghanistan. They would rather kill their female family members if they are thought to have committed wrongdoing than lose face in their community."

"Honor," as Afghans use the word, doesn't have the same meanings we would give it, behavior characterized by decency and honesty that brings public esteem and respect to a person. They don't even use it in the connotation of purity or chastity when applied to women (which is definition 7 in the 2015 *Merriam-Webster Dictionary*). "Honor," to Afghan men, is much more of a synonym for "women," particularly women of reproductive age seen as the property of their men. The further sense of treating a woman honorably—that is, not deceiving her sexually or romantically—is missing, which comes as a bit of a surprise considering how often honor is invoked in the treatment of women in Afghanistan.

The Dari word for "honor," *namoos*,[3] in the connotations we would give it, does not exist in the venerable Persian dictionary, the *Dekhoda*. Instead the only use of the word that has come down to Afghans as "honor," from that dictionary, means esteem and respect given for upholding and defending religious faith. Afghans do conflate honor with both religion and women, since they use religion as justification for their treatment of women (often on dubious theological grounds), but that layer of meaning is often lost as Afghans use "honor" today. Consider the notorious Article 398 of the Afghan Penal Code, which limits the punishment of *men* for murder to only two years' imprisonment for crimes of passion against women in their families. (There is no similar limitation of punishment for women who commit crimes of passion.) Article 398 says, as Kabul University law professor and women's activist Shahla Farid pointed out, that the punishment of men for murder is limited in cases where actions of the victims affect the man's honor, and it implicitly defines "their honor" as "including wives, sisters, daughters, nieces, aunts, mothers and other female relatives." In other words, as Dr. Farid translates it in Article 398, "honor" is legally defined as the women in a man's life over whom he has ownership or control. And that is how Afghans do use the term.[4]

When Afghan men say, as they often do, "We are a poor people, and all we have is our honor," what they are really saying is, "We are a poor people, and all we have is our women." Hence purdah and the Afghans' fanatical obsession with keeping their womenfolk out of public view. Hence the attitude that rape is not a crime, since women should never be in a position to be raped. If rape does happen, there has to have been some behavioral breakdown in the family of the victim; either the family did not keep her safe or she evaded their security.

I heard similar words from Zakia's father, Zaman, repeatedly. "I am a poor man. All I have is my honor." It was why it seemed logical to him to equate the loss of his daughter with the theft of one of his chickens; she was just a far more valuable piece of property.

Shortly after we met with Zaman, we went over to the village of Surkh Dar nearby and talked to Anwar, Ali's father, as well. We told Anwar about Zaman's intimate knowledge of the first days of their flight. Later Anwar related this information to Zakia and Ali, which persuaded them to set off on the run again. It seemed clear to them that Zakia's father knew someone who had seen them along the way, so it might not take him long to figure out that turning north at Azhdar village and heading back into the valley would have been much easier for an ill-equipped pair of fugitives than tackling the forbidding, snow-covered heights of sixteen-thousand-foot Shah Foladi.

Anwar was adamant that no previous marriage had ever taken place, that it was a ploy invented by a bitter father after the fact, but he was worried about the implications. Bigamy was both a crime and a terrible sin (for a woman, not a man, who can traditionally have four wives in Afghanistan), and Ali could be charged as well with kidnapping, a capital offense. In theory they could be stoned to death, because bigamy was also adultery.

Anwar tugged at his white beard nervously and asked if we could help Zakia and Ali.

Perhaps, if we could find them.

Jawad was convinced that the old man knew where they were and probably had Ali's current phone number as well but that he'd stopped trusting us when he realized we had also been talking to Zakia's family. He had come a long way from the angry father defending the cultural status quo, who beat his son for trying to bring dishonor on the community; just what had led to this transformation would take us a while to work out, but he had definitely taken Ali and Zakia's side.

The cris de coeur from *New York Times* readers had convinced me that we needed to bring the story up to date and raise its profile beyond just a print effort. Editors agreed and felt that now that the lovers were together, getting pictures of them with each other would be key to keeping interest high. People needed to see them together for them to become real; it was a love story as well as a look into the dark heart of a deeply disturbed society and the social and cultural obstacles that had prevented much meaningful progress on women's rights in Afghanistan. Without pictures the lovers' story would remain essentially abstract, lacking the power to move people—perhaps even someone who could do something to help. All we had was Mauricio Lima's portraits of the two of them, taken separately, so the paper assigned another photographer, in case we found them again, and a videographer to do a story on their romance and escape.[5]

That was all theoretical, since there could be no visuals unless we did find them, and no one was talking about where they might be. They had left their home village of Surkh Dar in secrecy shortly after our interviews with the fathers. First Zakia, at night in a full-length shawl, accompanied by Ali's mother, had taken a taxi to the town of Nayak Bazaar, the administrative center of the mountainous district of Yakawlang. A relative had agreed to put Zakia and Chaman up for one night, but not the couple together, who would be too easily spotted. The next night Ali and his father similarly took a taxi up to Nayak Bazaar, and Anwar left the couple together there. They had thought they would easily find a place to stay but realized that people had begun looking at them suspiciously. Separately they could evade detection, but together they were Zakia and Ali, and people could readily add it up. In these remote mountain places, every stranger sticks out.

The road they took up to Nayak Bazaar was a spanking-new, Japanese-built highway for the first forty miles or so, quite possibly the best road in the country for as long as it lasted. There had been an unusually large amount of snow late that winter, and in their flight they passed the newly groomed ski slopes on the flanks of the Koh-i-Baba range, which at the time were still being patronized by a smattering of late-season Western skiers.[6] The road between Bamiyan and Band-e-Amir is so good that there's even a Western-funded NGO[7] devoted to promoting women's cycling that uses it for bike touring, a sport previously unknown to Afghan women and rather awkward for someone in a burqa.

The paved road ended after Nayak Bazaar. With Zakia clutching two plastic bags of clothing and Ali a small backpack, they walked up a dirt road out of the town and then left it for a trail up into the mountains. That first night they ended up sleeping outdoors, with a fire beside the path, and then the next day they walked all day until they came to the village of Kham-e Bazargan, where they knew there was a home with distant relatives who had long ago been neighbors in Surkh Dar village. They had not realized how spread out Kham-e Bazargan was; it extended along the highway through the spectacular Yakawlang Gorge for miles, and the little market area was far from the homestead they sought. Ali had been there once, but many years before, and by car, not by foot. That night, rather than enter the market and run into the wrong person, they took refuge in a cave in an area so barren they could not find enough sticks for a fire. These mountains were not as high as the Koh-i-Baba, but they still rose up to fourteen thousand feet and in those first weeks of April were still partly snow-covered. The days were as sunny and mild as the nights were harsh and cold. After a second night in the cave, they finally found the home of Zahra and Haji Abdul Hamid, which sat on its own promontory above the Yakawlang River, in a steep gorge with towering mountains on either side.

It was a typical rural Afghan home, a compound surrounded by a wall of mud wattle that enclosed gardens and yards, with several interconnected mud-brick buildings that gave private areas for the wives of the sons and communal areas for the men. There were three other homes nearby in the tiny hamlet on that knoll, but they all belonged to close relatives. The hamlet could be seen from the main well-graded dirt road, but it was a mile's hike away, down into the bottomland, across the river on a shaky log bridge, and then back up the steep knoll on which the homestead stood.

Not for the first time, Zakia and Ali approached the home with no guarantee of what reception awaited them. They were former neighbors, distantly related like nearly everyone in their village, but still they had no way to know for sure how these people would react. Fortunately, when the couple related to Haji and Zahra what had happened to them the past couple weeks, the older couple readily agreed to give them refuge.

"At any home, when we were running, we would knock on the door and say, 'We are running because we're in love,' and usually they would take us in and help us," Ali said. "It was not because we were Hazaras and they were Hazaras. It's because everyone has at least once experienced love in their early lives, and they knew what it meant to be in love, even if they didn't have their love with them still. Even the governor, when Zakia-*jan* was in the shelter, she said, 'It's not because you're Hazara that I'm helping you but because she loves you and she shouldn't be without you.' "[8]

The house of Zahra and Haji was the first place where Zakia and Ali had felt safe since their flight from Bamiyan town. It, too, was a mud-brick dwelling, but the window frames were all of hand-planed lumber, painted a cheerful sky blue; the compound was freshly swept and as clean as a place with packed earthen floors could be. The roof was supported with battens of crooked birch trunks. In the bottomland wheat and potato seedlings were already sprouting, the green making a startling contrast with the dull brown and pale golden colors of the dirt slopes above. Higher on the mountainside, another green smudge had started to appear, a dusting of grass sprouts, watered by the still-melting snow. "It was good to begin a new life with greenery and spring," Ali later said. They took walks in the steep grazing lands, reminiscent of the slopes where they spent their childhoods together herding sheep. It was as close to a honeymoon as they were likely to have. "They seemed so happy together," Zahra said. "For the whole week they were here, they were never fighting or angry."

Then one day Zahra's children came home from school and said other kids had asked them who they were hiding. An old woman, another distant relative from Surkh Dar, heard what the schoolkids were saying. She stopped into Zahra's house on her way home and spotted the couple.

Haji told them they would have to leave soon; it was only a matter of time before word got from the old lady back to Surkh Dar and then to either Zakia's family in Kham-e-Kalak or to the authorities in Bamiyan town. That evening Ali climbed to the top of the mountain, where he was able to get a cell-phone signal, and called his father. He and Zakia were down to their last thousand afghanis, about twenty dollars, and out of places to go. Anwar was also nearly broke and could not afford the cost of a taxi to reach them. "Call the journalists," Ali said. "Maybe they can bring you to us." His father said he would try, but he wasn't at all sure he could trust us; he said he would also try to raise some money from relatives.

My colleague Jawad had been doggedly calling Anwar every day looking for news, and he reached him shortly after he spoke to his son. Anwar said he did not know for sure where his son was, but he was running out of money and he wanted to try to find him. He agreed to help us reach him in the hopes that our involvement in the case could get the couple out of the country. We were on the next morning's flight to Bamiyan. At the airstrip there we were met by our two most experienced *Times* office drivers, Fareed and Kabir, who had crossed the Hindu Kush from Kabul by car overnight; the risk of Taliban checkpoints was too great for any but the most foolhardy foreigners to travel by land. Fareed and Kabir took the precaution of stripping their cars, their persons, and the contents of their phones clean of association with foreigners; there have been occasions when the Taliban have murdered travelers in the Ghorband Valley route to the Shibar Pass simply for having dollars in their wallets rather than afghanis.

We set out early in the morning, picking up Anwar and his son Bismillah a mile outside of Surkh Dar, lest Zaman's family spot us, and began driving up into the heart of the central highlands. We were in two cars, with eight people including the drivers. Also with Jawad and me were Ben C. Solomon, a *Times* videographer[9] and Diego Ibarra Sánchez, a still photographer who was on assignment for us then. Anwar was cautious about telling us where we were going, and Jawad said it was clear that he still wasn't sure if he could trust us and was trying to decide whether he should. We shifted passengers around so Jawad and I could sit with the old man and Bismillah, and for the next couple of hours we set about trying to win Anwar's trust and confidence. We assured him we would never give away Zakia and Ali's location nor divulge his role or that of his sons in helping to hide them.

Stopping in Nayak Bazaar, we all had a breakfast of freshly baked loaves of round flatbread and oily eggs in a long, low room with plastic sheeting stretched in front of the windows to keep the sun's heat in, greenhouse style. Our presence in the bazaar, which was just a half-mile-long strip of shops along the muddy road, caused a commotion. Two carloads of foreigners were hardly low-profile; we might as well have been a traveling circus. We worked out with Anwar a plan to keep the photographers away from the couple's hiding place, once we found it, until we could discern if it was safe or not for the couple to join us—and whether they were willing and able to cooperate.

I had deep misgivings and a growing sense of guilt; it seemed likely that we would expose the couple if we did find them, without any guarantee that a more visual story about them would save their lives. In fact, the opposite could happen: It might make them easier for their pursuers to find. I thought about aborting it all but then thought that if the old man wanted us to come, it might be the right thing to do. This could not be great country to be a fugitive in for long; there just weren't enough places to hide unless you really were staying in caves, and for how long could they possibly do that? The remotest corners of Afghanistan were populated, if thinly, and they would have to go out to get water and food.

It was especially difficult for a woman to hide anywhere in this society. Amina, the teenager who was killed after fleeing her family's arranged marriage in Balkh Province,[10] was picked up by the police within an hour of her arrival, during daytime, at the bazaar in the provincial capital, Pul-e-Kumri. Bibi Aisha, sold as a child bride to a Taliban commander, fled when her husband was away fighting and went to the nearest market town, where police promptly picked her up and returned her to the family, even though in that area it would have been clear it was a Taliban family. She is the girl whose nose was cut off by that husband as punishment for having run away and later she was featured on the cover of *Time* magazine.[11] Even being with a man is sufficient camouflage only if the man is taken for a brother or husband, and Afghans are quick to sniff out ones who are not. When sixteen-year-old Soheila,[12] given away in marriage years before she was born to an elderly man, fled with her cousin Niaz Mohammad, the two were repeatedly stopped by police, even before her family pursued them. Policemen somehow could tell they weren't married.

How much harder it would be for the lovers to successfully flee with foreigners in their vicinity. In the course of our search for them, we were conspicuous as probably the only Westerners within a hundred miles. For several hours we wended our way up the Yakawlang Gorge, a place of spectacular but forbidding views and only this one dusty road, no side roads at all for many miles at a stretch. When we reached Kham-e Bazargan and the homestead where they were hiding, Anwar continued to insist on the fiction that he did not know where they were. Instead he said he would go and ask directions from that distant homestead on the little knoll, a mile off the highway. Worried that if they *were* hiding there, our presence would surely give them away, I told the drivers to split up our cars a little, parking a mile apart, and persuaded the photographers to keep their gear and themselves out of sight. For them this long trip without the prospect of a single frame was a bitter pill, which both Ben and Diego took with a mixture of equanimity and frustration.

Anwar and Bismillah came back at a trot. This indeed was where the pair were hiding, and Zakia was still there—but not Ali. The night before, Haji had told them they would have to leave today; Ali took off before dawn—they weren't sure where to, but probably he hitchhiked to the next village, three hours' drive away. Haji had gone in pursuit, furious that Ali had not taken Zakia with him as Haji had asked. He took the minibus he owns, which plies the mountain roads as an informal, private bus service. As bad as all that was, it was a godsend that solved our conundrum: the worry that we would inadvertently give away the couple's location and compromise their safety. We had found them just as they were in the process of eviction, and that had nothing to do with us.

Zakia refused to come out even to talk to us, however, until her husband returned—even with her father-in-law, Anwar, there. We sat down with Anwar and Zahra to wait and to discuss what had transpired. "I'm deeply concerned. They have to go now, I did it just for God's sake to help them," Zahra said. "I support what they did—they love each other—but the problem is if it comes to a dispute between families, they might kill each other, and they might kill us, too. They might kill them and cut them into pieces."

Haji returned, having been unable to find Ali, but friends had called him to say that Nayak Bazaar was full of rumors that the pair were hiding in his place; they told him he should expect the police to arrive soon to apprehend them. "The police could arrest all of us for this," he said, apologetic but adamant. "Now they're calling it a kidnapping." He wanted us to leave immediately, taking Zakia with us. But she refused to emerge from the women's quarters, Zahra was not going to force her, and none of the men would dare enter. I promised Haji we would take them with us the moment Ali returned, which then put us in the uncomfortable position of providing them with getaway cars, but there seemed to be no alternative. I justified it by saying that we would use the car journey as a means to interview and photograph them in safety, which we could no longer do at Haji's house without putting them all at risk of arrest. I was also uncomfortably aware that we were stepping over that line that separates journalists and their subjects. We were becoming part of the story, whatever we might tell ourselves; more accurately, whatever *I* might tell myself and, as the person in charge, compel the others to go along with.

While we waited, Zahra told us about her hopes for her six children, who were all in school; her eldest, an eighteen-year-old, Ahmed Zia, was first in his class in twelfth grade, wanted to go to university to become an engineer, and was proud that he'd just been able to vote in the presidential election for the first time. (When we later spoke to Ahmed Zia, he was contemptuous about Ali and Zakia. "What they did was wrong," he said. He would never tolerate one of his young sisters behaving like that, he said. But neither would he give Zakia and Ali away, out of respect for his parents.) Zahra herself could read and write but had only a few years of school; her husband was a schoolteacher as well as a landowner. None of this could have been possible in Afghanistan a decade ago; in fact, Zakia and Ali could not have been possible, Zahra said. If today they were pursued by society and its laws, it was only the fault of ignorant, uneducated people like their neighbor. "That stupid woman," Zahra kept calling her.

So much had changed since the Taliban time, Zahra mused, when she taught her daughters in secrecy in her home, since the Taliban had closed all the girls' schools.[13] Now they could study openly, and the Hazara girls in their community did so. They could watch Bollywood love stories on television and listen to romantic music on radios and mobile telephones, which also had all been forbidden. Yet they still lived in the shadow of that time. The Taliban had injected something new and malevolent into Afghanistan's intensely private culture: the concept that honor, as it applied to women, was not an issue just for the man whose honor was at stake, the man who owned those women. Instead it was something that concerned everyone; not only the state but every man had the obligation to enforce honor, as he saw it. The Taliban had gone, but the intrusive attitude of its notorious Ministry for the Promotion of Virtue and Suppression of Vice was left behind, among people like "that awful woman," as Zahra called her. Or, for that matter, among the Bamiyan police, who were then pursuing an eighteen-year-old for the supposed crime of fleeing a place where she was staying legally and voluntarily.

Anwar sat cross-legged, alternately dialing his son's cell phone and looking out the window. The photographer, Diego, was restless and had disappeared; later we discovered he'd gone into the kitchen, in the women's quarters, and found Zakia, posing her under a beam of sunlight coming through a chimney hole in the mud roof. Diego was fond of his sunbeams and was forever trying to find them in the dark dwellings of Afghanistan. He said he hadn't understood that men were not allowed in the women's quarters; it was a serious cultural breach, one that could easily get a man killed in the wrong house. Diego's English was semifluent but spotty; it was hard to be sure what he didn't understand, versus what he chose not to understand if it got in the way of a picture.

I asked Anwar how it came to pass that, having beaten his son for starting his affair with Zakia, he now was going to the ends of the earth for him. "It is true that I punished him then, but now I have changed my mind. It happened because I saw that my daughter-in-law stood behind my son and was brave enough to say she loves my son, and now it is an honor for us to stand behind her," he said.

Zahra teared up listening to him.

"Now she is a part of my family, she is my own daughter. She is a part of my family now, and I would do anything for her as well as for him. Even more for her." As an answer it was pretty unsatisfactory, little better than a handy if heartfelt slogan. It was more likely that once Zakia's family began publicly denouncing their son and threatening his life, Anwar's pride and that of his sons was challenged, and perhaps that pushed them to rally to his side. Zaman's pride wanted to see his daughter dead; Anwar's pride would see his daughter-in-law honored instead.

About midafternoon Ali finally showed up, his arrival heralded by half a dozen children from the compound who had staked out the path from the road; again he had hitchhiked. It turned out he had gone to a village farther up the highway where he thought he could contact us by cell phone; instead we had by then reached his hiding place, where *our* phones only worked from the hilltops.

His ringtone that day, which we heard sometimes when we climbed the slopes to call him, praying we would get through to him before the police arrived, was a Pashto love song by Latif Nangarhari:

> *Come here, my little flower, come!*
> *Let me tear open my breast*
> *And show you my own heart, naked.*[14]

It was an emotional few minutes as Zakia packed Ali's bag for him and gathered her own plastic bags into one larger sack. We explained that we would give them a ride to the nearest safe place and wanted to interview them and photograph them on the journey as we went, so long as we could do it without compromising them further. They were strangely quiet and calm, even oddly cheerful at the prospect of this next leg of the run, while everyone else was taking it hard. They understood that there was no other course of action; everyone else felt complicit in forcing it upon them.

I asked Zakia why she did not wear the all-covering burqa to disguise herself as they fled, and she laughed scornfully. "I will not put that thing on me," she said. Similarly, I was surprised that Ali had not changed his look at all; his hair was still full, brushed up in the front and slicked back, and he had not grown out his beard much, one of the easiest things to do in a society where beards are commonplace, more so than clean-shaven faces. He laughed. "She would never agree to look at me if I did that." It was too cheerful a moment; one wanted to grab these kids and say, *Hey, you won't be choosing your haircuts and dress in jail.* They did agree, however, that they would change their costumes in the next day or two, so that their colorful outfits, especially hers, would not be so easily recognized from any published pictures.

Diego had spotted another ray of light shining through a hole in the roof somewhere and wanted to delay our departure to get both of them in it, but we insisted on giving him no more than a minute and then bolting. Ben had already run ahead so he could get in front of them for footage of them heading down from the promontory, finally together and really fleeing. The lovers held hands, unbidden, as they walked, and when they came to what passed for a footbridge—three spindly, skinny birch trunks laid across the rushing river, so thin they bounced at every step—they crossed one by one, Zakia not even bothering to take off her high heels. The rest of us crossed gingerly and awkwardly in our Gore-Tex boots, worried about all those phones and cameras falling with us into the icy torrent below.

Before we piled into the cars, I slipped Ali a thousand dollars when no one else was looking. He had never asked for it, but neither did he question it, just tucked it into his shirt. I did it on impulse, although I'd been thinking of it earlier; I made sure none

of my colleagues saw me. It was all money that various readers had
pledged, even begged me to pass on to the couple, I reasoned, and
they would follow through on those pledges in time, no doubt.
And if they didn't . . . well, it seemed the least I could do. Ali's last
thousand afghanis were not going to get them far, to be sure.

Much more of an issue than the money, journalistically, was
abetting their escape. It was one thing to talk to them and photograph them on the run, but we were now providing the getaway
cars. Once we put them in the cars with us, the die was cast; I was no
longer just an observer but in a pretty important way a participant.
The money could be dismissed as a humanitarian gesture, like giving money to a starving family while reporting in a miserable refugee camp—who wouldn't? This, however, was helping people flee
criminal charges placed against them by their government. There
was no chance to ask my bosses what they would think about this,
but that was just as well, since I suspect I know what the answer
would have been and I would not have been able to obey it. Zakia
and Ali were here in part—I would come to realize how much a
part—because of us. As the reader had said, "You're responsible for
them now." What else could we do? We had the only cars avail-
able in Kham-e Bazargan; Haji's minibus was out on its rounds. So
should we have waited there until the police arrived and then photographed their arrest? How cynical and exploitative that would
have been. It came down to this choice: abandon your principles
and stick to your humanity or stick to your principles and abandon
your humanity. True, documenting their arrest would have been
the better story, dramatically speaking, but who could live with
that? We all felt uneasy about it, but I told Ben and Diego, "Look,
if we work with them here, they won't want to cooperate, because
they need to be running. If they run into the hills, we won't be
able to stay with them for long. If we put them in our cars, we'll
be able to work with them in some privacy and security." Which
was all true, to a point, but it was still an equivocation.

Later we would learn that the police arrived at Haji and Zahra's
that evening, only hours behind us. They might well have passed
us on the road, lost to sight in the dust swirls our cars stirred up.

On the long drive down to Nayak Bazaar, we had time to talk with the couple about their flight so far, and I asked if it had been worth it, escaping from the women's shelter and eloping. "Yes, it's worth it because we love each other," Ali said.

"If we had only had one day together, it would have been worth it," Zakia said. "How can I be sad? We're together. I'm with my love."

One thing that became clear talking to both of them was that their time on the run had convinced them they had no long-term future in their own country; they said they had decided that their ultimate solution would be to flee abroad.

Then Jawad and I swapped cars, letting the photographers have some time with Zakia and Ali for the rest of the ride. Ben was happy to interview and video them inside the car, but Diego wanted them outside again, against the dramatic backdrop of the barren mountain landscape.

"Look, Diego, we're on the run," I said. "The cops are searching for them. Half the country is talking about them. You can't possibly shoot them outside the car."

He was insistent, and I finally gave in a little. "But only if the road is empty and then only for three minutes, no more."

Our car was in front, some distance ahead of them, and when we arrived on the outskirts of Nayak Bazaar, we realized that the second car with Zakia, Ali, Ben, and Diego inside was nowhere to be seen and was a lot more than three minutes behind us. We doubled back, only to find Diego posing them on top of a hillock, a fair walk from the road but in clear view of anyone who came along. I often wonder how differently it all would have ended if they'd been captured there and then by that carload of police on their way back from where we'd just been, because one of us had been too journalistically eager for yet another piece of the story.

I took over the lovers' car and banished Diego to the other one. We carried on into the town, dropping the couple at the top of a side street that headed off into the mountain up a jeep track. It was nearly dark. Another two hours' walk from there would take them to a safe house, one they had used once before, and after that they would set off across the mountains for Wardak, now that they had enough money to find a driver with a jeep, and then find buses to take them to southern Ghazni Province, to one of the Hazara communities in that otherwise dangerous province. Ben Solomon wanted to follow them.

"Out of the question," I said. "How could they possibly escape with a big white American tagging along?"

My story ran in the *Times* three days later, on April 22, along with the video[15] by Ben on our website, and Diego's stills,[16] which were so good that his presumptive perfidy had to be forgiven. The cumulative effect was to take a terrific story that already had generated a great deal of interest and increase that manifold.

The print story[17] had a suitably nonspecific dateline, "HINDU KUSH RANGE, AFGHANISTAN," a large area that traversed more than a third of the country. It ended:

> They hoped to be hundreds of miles away by Saturday morning, but were not sure which way they would go. The road to the north went through Taliban country. To the west, bandit country, where they risked being robbed—or worse. The road to the south went over passes still blocked by snow.
>
> There was no road east, but they could always walk.

That was a bit of protective obfuscation. Their real plan was to wait for the snows to melt to the south and then make it over the passes to Wardak Province: Taliban country but also Hazara country. Before they took their leave, I told them I didn't think they could keep hiding in these barren, unforested mountains; every stranger was a subject of suspicion. Two youthful strangers in love and on the run were a red flag.

"Give it a few weeks, then come to Kabul," I said. With five million people in the city, there had to be somewhere they could find to disappear among them. But then what right did I have to be giving Zakia and Ali advice?

6

❧

# MYSTERY BENEFACTOR

Zakia and Ali were saved again and again by the kindnesses of strangers. Villagers who sheltered them on the run. Passersby who spotted them and chose not to call the police. Journalists who wrote about them and made it harder to dispose of them—not just ourselves but also many Afghan journalists who had picked up the story. Women's advocates who lobbied on their behalf in the face of official disapproval. Then there were the strangers all over the world, but particularly in the United States, who were moved enough by their story to try to do something about it, readers who both encouraged and sometimes shamed me into keeping on their case and later became contributors whose money, mostly in modest donations, kept the couple going. When you're on the run, poverty is a potent enemy.

There were hundreds of such readers who reached out. An American named Walker Moore wondered if he couldn't pay a bride price that would make Zakia and Ali's match acceptable to both their families; Walker Moore turned out to be a *nom de pinceau* of two collaborative painters, John Walker and Roxann Moore; the Zakia-and-Ali story reminded them of their own union, which had been bitterly opposed by Roxann's conservative Southern Baptist family in Texas, Mr. Walker said. Adele Goldberg, a professor of psychology at Princeton University, offered to make a donation to help relocate the couple. Dr. Douglas Fleming, a physician and cancer researcher from Princeton, offered to donate a hundred dollars a month to them for a year to cover their expenses on the run, and his later donations proved critically helpful. E. Jean Carroll, who wrote a relationship advice column for *Elle* magazine and also runs a matchmaking service, Tawkify.com, offered them "airfare to the US, a chaperone for Zakia, and a place for them to stay"— until they were married. She, too, later sent money that helped in their escape. Beth Goodman also offered to host them in the United States. Many had vaguer but also heartfelt requests. "I'm French, I'm a woman and I live on the same planet," wrote Louisa Roque. "How can we help their parents to open their minds and hearts?"

The response went ballistic after we finally had both photographs and video of them together to accompany the words. It was gratifying that we'd touched a nerve and moved so many people. I no longer felt that this was a case that lay outside the boundaries of hope. At the same time, it was frustrating. Helping Zakia and Ali stay on the run was no more sustainable in the long term than many of the other things that well-intentioned Westerners have been doing for Afghans, whether paying them salaries ten times the Afghan norm[1] or providing their military with steeply subsidized fuel, much of it diverted to the black market.[2] There was little that anyone could do to help the couple in any permanent way unless a government stepped in and made it possible for them to leave their country. For those countries that might have been so inclined, that was politically difficult—in part because of popular backlashes against immigration in many Western countries and in part because so many of those countries needed to show skeptics back home that Afghanistan was improving on human rights and merited their continued national investment. With criminal charges hanging over the lovers, it became diplomatically awkward and contradictory for countries that had donated so much money to rule-of-law development work in Afghanistan to then turn around and say they had no confidence in the Afghan justice system, however many flat-earthers wielded its gavels. The United States alone had by 2014 spent more than $1.2 billion on rule-of-law programming[3] to do things like train judges and promote equal rights for women.

President Hamid Karzai could always choose to step in and pardon them or order the charges dropped. But this was even more of a long shot; Karzai's wife, an obstetrician before their marriage, had rarely been seen in public afterward and no longer practiced her profession.[4] Once seen as a champion of women's rights, Mr. Karzai was now widely viewed by most women's activists as having betrayed their cause.

While there was little these readers could do to help the couple directly, their money could buy some breathing room, and it soon began accumulating in the account of Women for Afghan Women[5] after I began answering reader mail with this note:

> Dear Readers,
>
> Pardon the impersonal e-mail but so many people have written me about the Afghan lovers that I can't answer everyone right away, although I aim to do so eventually.
>
> Many of you have asked how you could help and, previously, I haven't had a satisfactory answer.
>
> However, now a well-respected and long-established organization, Women for Afghan Women, has decided to start a fund dedicated to assisting the couple. The group's executive director, Manizha Naderi, has assured us that 100 percent of any donations to that fund will be passed directly to the couple.
>
> . . . .
>
> I feel sure that WAW has the means and the capacity to get donations to them personally.
>
> With warm regards,

Some people had taken the initiative even earlier and sent money to a trusted accountant to deliver to Zakia and Ali, which,

I had quietly had assured a few of the more persistent among them, would be a safe way to do it. Before that money could clear from the bank for the accountant to deal with, however, we had rushed off to our rendezvous with Zakia and Ali up in the mountains in Yakawlang, so it had been my own money I gave them, telling myself I was just fronting it temporarily. WAW later made donations to them easy and efficient, and the group was beyond any reproach; it was undoubtedly the most effective NGO in Afghanistan fighting for women's rights on a basic, practical level and the biggest operator of women's shelters.[6] WAW's seven main shelters are in some of the country's most difficult areas. It also runs family-reconciliation and counseling centers and homes for children whose mothers are in prison. Eventually the *Times* ran a notice on its website telling people how they could donate to help the couple. The money that came in was not huge, a few thousand dollars, partly because I advised donors who asked how much to give that large sums of money were not necessary and might be distorting or cause problems in their own right. In Afghan terms the donations were adequate to keep the couple alive and help finance a safe place for them to hide. I suspect this was the first time the *New York Times* had in effect encouraged its readers to send money to criminal fugitives, which is technically and legally what Zakia and Ali were, however bogus the charges against them. Editors in New York were as moved by the story of the Afghan lovers as everyone else was.

If only we could find Zakia and Ali to let them know about all these offers of help. For quite a while, they were not aware that a fund-raising drive was under way on their behalf. Since we had left them in Nayak Bazaar in late April, there had been no word from them at all, and Ali's phone went unanswered, sounding not so much as a lovesick ringtone. His father and brothers said they had heard from him and thought he was in Ghazni Province or maybe Wardak, they weren't sure. He called them when he had a signal; they couldn't really call him, and of course nor could we. I was beginning to think that they had gone ahead and fled to Iran, and if they had, the story ended there—my story and possibly their story. Iran would be a dead end in almost every respect. While there are

950,000 legally registered Afghan refugees in Iran, according to the UN High Commissioner for Refugees[7] the real number is as much as three times that, most of them living there illegally.[8] The Iranian government has long since stopped granting refugee status to new arrivals, so all those who have arrived in recent years are undocumented illegals, without even the limited rights afforded refugees and guaranteed by international conventions and United Nations agencies. They cannot legally work, have no civil rights, cannot send their children to school—and could never be legally resettled to a third country.[9] At any moment they could be forcibly deported back to Afghanistan, and they often are. Some are killed and their bodies returned to the nearest border post with no explanation from the Iranian authorities. For Afghan refugees, just getting to Iran could be a dangerous crossing through forbidding deserts, far worse than anything Mexican and Central American immigrants face in the American Southwest. And since an American journalist could not follow refugees to Iran, there would likely be nothing more I could do for them and little more to write about them. The only thing Iran had in its favor as a destination was language; Farsi or Persian, the language spoken in Iran, and Dari, which Ali and Zakia spoke, are nearly as mutually intelligible as British and American English.

Finally, late in April, Ali called us; they could be in Kabul the next day, he said, if it was okay with us. He wanted assurances they would be safe there, and we told him that the big city could give them anonymity they would never find elsewhere, and there was donor money waiting to help them with expenses. Two days later Zakia and Ali arrived with his brother Bismillah and moved into the home of his aunt, his father's sister, who lived not far from the old city in central Kabul, in a neighborhood of squatters' buildings erected on the steep slopes of the Chindawul Hill.

Historically, Kabul had been settled on a flat plateau with several small mountains that jut up singly from the plain, but in the past decade its population had increased from less than a million to more than 5 million residents, and squatters had moved higher and higher on the steep slopes of places like Chindawul that were once viewed as uninhabitable, carving small plots out of the rock and filling the reclaimed space with slapdash cinder- and mud-block constructions.

With no services but electricity, if that, such homes were cheaper the higher up the hill they were located. The aunt's house was a one-room shack made of mud brick and concrete, reached by a fifteen-minute climb up an already steep dirt path, which soon becomes *so* steep that it's replaced by a nearly vertical stone staircase, with two hundred fifty steps to reach the aunt's house. The entire dwelling was no bigger than an American-size bedroom, with a primitive latrine and a gas burner and a bowl for a kitchen; a curtain hung across the room to give the couple some privacy. They stowed their few possessions, mostly just clothing, in the plastic bags they'd carried them in; at first they didn't even have mattresses to sleep on, just fake-bamboo mats. The nearest water was at the foot of the hill, and they hauled it in a pair of big plastic jerry cans, like those used for gasoline, slung across their shoulders at either end of a stout stick.

Although Chindawul was a safely Hazara neighborhood, Jawad and I decided not to draw attention to Zakia and Ali by meeting them there. Instead we arranged to meet Ali alone, reasoning that they were easier to recognize as a couple than singly. We would pick him up outside the Pamir Cinema, at the foot of the hill, one of the few places he knew in the city. Half an hour before the meeting, Ali called to tell us his brother Bismillah had gone ahead to the meeting place to check it out and saw one of Zakia's older brothers on the street nearby. Did we know anything about that?

Of course we didn't, but our meeting was canceled and Ali again stopped answering his phone when we called. Another week went by before we were able to make a meeting happen, and then only by calling his father and persuading him that we had no reason to expose them to risk; spotting the brother there was just bad luck—or good luck that they saw him first and not the other way around. If that brother was in Kabul, he was probably working as a day laborer, and the Pamir Cinema is a common meeting place for laborers looking for day work, so in the future it would probably be a good place for us to avoid.

The night before, E. Jean Carroll, the advice columnist, had e-mailed to let me know she had done something that had never occurred to me would work—she sent money to Ali via Western Union. She gave me the coded number of the money wire to pass along to him so he could collect it. We relayed the details via Anwar, hoping that the prospect of receiving money would reassure Ali we were on his side.

I let Rabbi Shmuley know that Ali had come to Kabul, as I did several of the other well-wishers. Shmuley activated the fixer we had found him, Aimal Yaqubi, but Aimal had no more luck getting through to Ali than we had earlier. While we were waiting to meet with Ali, though, Shmuley had come up with a plan. He was outraged at how hard this had become. He'd gone straight to Samantha Power, the United States representative to the United Nations, and tried to persuade her that she had to push the American government to save the couple. By his account she had in turn persuaded the U.S. secretary of state, John Kerry, to try to do something, but despite their efforts both finally had come to the conclusion that they could not force the American government to change its policies and issue the couple a humanitarian visa to save them from persecution. With criminal charges against them, and the United States supposedly an ally of Afghanistan, taking them directly out of the country would mean using the visa system to help Afghans escape their own, American-financed criminal-justice system. They would have to resolve their case first, legally, or they would have to get to another country and apply for a visa there, a process that Shmuley said he was told would take them six months or more even with Samantha Power behind it.

Shmuley had come up with a novel work-around. He said he'd been in touch with his good friend President Paul Kagame of Rwanda and that Mr. Kagame would issue visas to Ali and Zakia and would let them stay as his guests for as long as it would take for them to get visas to go on to America, a process that Rabbi Shmuley said Samantha Power promised to expedite—provided the couple were out of Afghanistan. This would be financed through Mr.

Shmuley's World Values Network, using money from a mystery benefactor: a very wealthy woman, as he had said.

Not only did it seem a bizarre solution, but there was a serious complication. As it stood then, only Ali had his identity card, or *tazkera,* which was required in order to get a passport; Zakia's father had possession of her *tazkera* and was not about to give it up. So she could not even apply for a passport, and Ali would have to do so at the risk of being arrested on the outstanding bigamy and kidnapping charges.

"How hard can it be to get passports?"

"Not hard at all, if you're not worried about the FCPA."

The meaning of those initials was immediately clear: the Foreign Corrupt Practices Act, which makes it a federal crime for American citizens to pay bribes in foreign countries, even where it's a standard and locally accepted practice. His mystery benefactor would want none of that, Shmuley said. The couple would have to find a way to obtain passports legally, without getting caught on the outstanding criminal charges.

That was not hopeless, since both of them had fairly common first names—Mohammad Ali was his; he had no surname, like many rural Afghans. Zakia, too, had no surname,[10] which is even more common among women. (Kept in purdah, women have even less need of a full name than men.) So if the couple went to the passport office one at a time, that might possibly work. There was a risk in it, to be sure, especially if no officials could be bribed.

Finally, after two weeks of ducking us, Ali, out of money, agreed to meet us outside a hospital in a busy part of town. We picked him up and took him to the Ché restaurant, in the Kart-e-Seh neighborhood, which passes for upscale in Kabul. The Ché is one of a type of Afghan restaurant, rarely frequented by foreigners, in which the tables are traditional raised platforms with cushions, each in a separate enclosure arranged around a central garden. Each has room for half a dozen people; with thatched roofs, thick vines, and screening around the sides, they are very private spaces. The ostensible purpose is to provide a place for families to dine in seclusion, so the women cannot be seen by others, and they do function that way. With a cooperative management, they also provide privacy for couples and mixed groups of unrelated people, and are often full of young people willing to defy social convention, courting and even, on occasion, necking. It was a perfect place for us to sit down with Ali away from prying eyes.

Ali had changed little since we'd last seen him nearly a month before; he was still beardless, his hair still in a pompadour, a style that stood out in Kabul. He was restless and nervous, and every few minutes his phone rang on silent and he looked at it with concern. I filled him in on what we knew. There was an Afghan employee at the American embassy who had been assigned to speak to him about their case, and we programmed the number into his phone so that he would recognize it when it rang and know it was okay to answer. We told him there was a wealthy American who wanted to help him and Zakia, who had enlisted an Afghan fixer to be their go-between, and we programmed Aimal Yaqubi's number into his phone as well. He had trouble understanding why we were introducing Aimal into the matter, though I explained that as a journalist I couldn't act on behalf of someone trying to find a solution for him. "But we trust you, and we only want to talk to you. We know you will help us," he said. It was hard to explain the notion of professional distance in any way that made sense to him, all the more so since it had begun to ring false to me.

While we talked, Ali was skittish and scarcely touched the food we ordered. When we told him about Shmuley's plan to get them to Rwanda, as a way station en route to America, he looked at us blankly. I realized we had to back up and start with some basic geography; he had only the vaguest idea of other countries, let alone other continents. A map to him was a meaningless piece of paper with strange lines on it. He had never seen an African or any black person; the only foreigners he'd ever seen were the European troops who helped train his army unit in Farah, and the first foreigner he'd ever seen up close was me. From time to time, I'd catch him looking at me sidewise, as if trying to figure out what manner of beast this could be or what I was up to, really. After a long explanation about Africa—how far away it was, how different

the climate, culture, and language, where it was located in relation
to the United States—he said he understood, but it was clear he
really did not. I didn't begin to try to explain Rwanda and what
that country specifically is like. "Whatever Africa is, that would be
better than hiding in caves," he said.

We told him that Women for Afghan Women had been receiving donations from people in the United States who'd read about
the couple's case and wanted to help them. The organization was
interested in giving him a lawyer who would fight their criminal
case for them, and would he want to talk to the lawyer? He refused;
as far as he was concerned, WAW was an organization that ran shelters, and shelters were bad. They would try to get Zakia to go into
one, and she would be a prisoner there again indefinitely. On this
there was no reasoning with him; no use pointing out that Zakia
would have been long dead without the Bamiyan shelter, whatever
her complaints about it. He would not consent to go to WAW's office himself to pick up money from the donors, for fear they would
somehow detain him; he wanted us to do it for him, but we refused.
His cell phone rang again, and this time he answered it and had a
fraught conversation with Zakia. She was worried about him, he
said, and when he hadn't answered her earlier calls, she'd grown
alarmed that something had happened. She knew that her brothers
were in town, and though Kabul was a city of 5 million people, its
size was beyond their imagining; it was as remote and foreign to
them as Africa would be.

We asked him if he had collected the three hundred dollars that
E. Jean Carroll had sent in the name of Ali, care of any Western
Union office in Kabul, but he had not. We realized that Anwar
was innumerate, though he'd said, out of embarrassment and po-
liteness, that he could take down the coded number needed to
collect the money. So we wrote it down for Ali and said we could
take him to one of the transfer offices; there are many of them at-
tached to Afghan banks. Ali was fine with numbers on a telephone,
but written down on paper they were just so many hieroglyphics.
Jawad would have to go along to help him.

We chose a Western Union office on Darulaman Road because

it was on a busy street but set back from the road. This particular bank had been the target of a Taliban suicide bomber the year before, in an attack that had killed a dozen people; many of the walls still had scooped-out patches from the shrapnel, and the windows were cardboarded over. It was ready for the next attack; unlike lightning, suicide bombers often strike the same place twice, and the office's entry was obscured by sandbagged blast walls and HESCOs, huge metal mesh containers filled with earth. It was menacing but private. The Western Union clerk confirmed they had the money, under that code number, but Ms. Carroll had sent it to first name Mohammad, last name Ali, and as far as the bank was concerned, his documents said he was first name Mohammad Ali, no last name. It's a common problem in Afghanistan, where more than half the population gets by with only one name.[11] I relayed this to Ms. Carroll, who corrected the first wire, sending a second payment immediately. By the next day, Zakia and Ali had three hundred dollars, enough money to live on, by the courtesy of an American stranger who had simply been moved by their story. From Ali and Zakia's point of view, three hundred dollars was enough to get by on for a month, and they remained adamant that WAW was off-limits, though the organization by now held several thousand dollars in donations for them.

Ali was being uncooperative journalistically as well. Our video department wanted to do a follow-up of the piece that Ben Solomon had shot in Yakawlang. Our photo desk wanted to shoot them again, too, and send a still photographer along whenever there was a new development in their case. We were constantly bombarded by requests from Afghan journalists who also wanted to follow their case; we didn't like turning our colleagues down, and this was, after all, a story about Afghan society that Afghans needed to hear. Ali was adamant, though, that they wanted no further photography, and he did not even want his wife to talk to us anymore. They also wanted no part of the Afghan press. It was too dangerous, he felt, and it was hard to argue with that.

His attitude was not going to help us keep interest in the couple high enough to force some sort of resolution. In journalism the great stories are the ones that can bring about change. This one could change the lives of two people who otherwise had no real prospects and perhaps give some real encouragement to others like them. But increasingly my subjects seemed to want nothing to do with us if they could not see the immediate practical benefit. I tried to persuade them that cases like theirs rarely end well when kept far from public view. I could not keep their story alive if a half of it, Zakia, was no longer speaking to me. Ali claimed he understood that, but then all that he would agree to, and only reluctantly, was to arrange for Zakia to speak to us on the phone from their hiding place. That's where we had to leave it for the time being.

Shmuley called me nearly nightly in those days, worried that his fixer was having trouble persuading Ali to meet with him. I said we had done as much as we could. I suggested that Aimal should go easy; we, too, had backed off, so Zakia and Ali did not feel pressured. Meanwhile Shmuley was also in touch with Fatima Kazimi, as was E. Jean Carroll, and Fatima was regaling them both with her own tale of woe.

I heard about this firsthand when Fatima arrived in Kabul late in April. She bustled into the *New York Times* compound in Wazir Akbar Khan, the diplomatic quarter of Kabul, dressed in her usual purple head scarf and the modesty trench coat favored by many Afghan women in official life. Fatima was not happy. She had just seen a translated copy of my latest article on the lovers, published April 22,[12] and was outraged that it focused on the couple and did not mention Fatima's role in the case. "I expected you to write about me," she said. "I brought them to you." In fact, the first article did mention Fatima prominently, quoted her at length, related her role in getting Zakia to the safety of the shelter—all things that were corroborated by many witnesses in Bamiyan, including several people who'd been in the court. Fatima just wasn't the central figure in that piece, nor should she have been. She had already complained to me then that she was disappointed that the first article made it a Romeo-and-Juliet love story and not a Fatima Kazimi rescue story. Then, when they had eloped, my March 31 article[13] had revisited the issue of Fatima's role, appropriately, since some were accusing her of engineering Zakia's breakout. Again Fatima was not the focus; the lovers were.

Now Fatima wanted us to set the matter straight and write another article about how terribly she had been treated in this affair. She claimed to have fled to Kabul with her entire family because she could no longer endure the many threats she was receiving in Bamiyan. She claimed to have lost her job at the women's ministry. "The entire village of the girl's father filed a complaint against me and accused me of helping Zakia escape—or helping Ali kidnap her, as they put it," she said. "I actually didn't do anything." She purportedly did help by allowing Zakia to get a telephone from Ali while she was in the shelter,[14] but Ali and Zakia both deny she had anything to do with that—although she did allow them to have a chaperoned meeting in the shelter at one point. "Whether I say I did help or did not help, everything comes back to me from the beginning," Fatima said. "I stepped in and stopped the court from doing something terrible. Yesterday her family members came to my former home in Bamiyan, looking for me, but I had moved. My life is in danger, and I am under threat. If I don't leave the country, something may happen to me or my family." She had four children, teenagers and young adults, and a husband. "You need to write that."

I was starting to have a hard time believing any of this, thinking that perhaps Fatima had gamed this whole thing from the beginning. I was shocked to discover that she had persuaded E. Jean Carroll to send money to help protect her. Fatima was earnestly depicting her case as more dire—and more important—than that of Zakia and Ali, who really *were* in danger of being killed (as Fatima herself had pointed out from the beginning). "Only the governor is on my side now, and how long can the governor defend me?" she said.

The governor of Bamiyan has executive authority over all the provincial government offices, save the courts; he controls the police force, so he can prevent arrests, order interventions, provide bodyguards, and so forth. He is a Hazara, like Fatima, and it's an overwhelmingly Hazara place; if anyone were likely to be in danger there now, it would be Zakia's Tajik family members, whose opposition to the marriage on ethnic and religious grounds would expose them to the anger of their more numerous Hazara neighbors. Zakia and Ali were at risk of violence at their hands, no doubt, but Fatima?

She was insistent, though, and I said we would write about the case again and probably mention her as well; in a piece a couple of days later,[15] I noted the role she had in alerting us to the case. Who was I to say, really, what the truth was in the matter? Maybe she *had* received death threats and was frightened by them and honestly felt that the only hope was to leave Afghanistan.

It certainly was true that anyone connected with sheltering women in Afghanistan was under intense pressure. Just the year before, the case of Bibi Aisha had contributed to a backlash against women's shelters after a picture showing that her nose had been cut off appeared on *Time*'s cover. Bibi Aisha was widely criticized in Afghanistan after that cover picture[16]—including by officials in the office of President Hamid Karzai—for bringing shame to her homeland, and she now lives with a foster family in Virginia, spurned in her own land and not only by the Taliban. The subsequent crackdown against women's shelters was led by prominent conservatives[17] who accused the shelters of undermining traditional values, promoting adulterous conduct, and even fronting for prostitution. One television network, Noorin TV, sent its star "investigative reporter," Nastoh Naderi, to the Women for Afghan Women shelter.[18] Denied entry, he stood in front of the gate and had his crew film men as they walked in. The men were guards who were employed by the shelter, working in the compound but not in the building that housed the women clients. On air Mr. Naderi described the guards as johns coming to patronize the prostituted women inside. The government then tried to take control of the women's shelters, all of which were run by either private charities or the United Nations, but was forced by an international outcry to back off and instead instituted regulations controlling their activities, under the purview of the Ministry of Women's Affairs.[19]

Fatima continued to insist she was under threat from Zakia's family. I had talked to Zakia's relatives, met some of her brothers and cousins and her father, and their determination to pursue vengeance made them worrisomely dangerous. But they had never expressed to me a desire to get back at Fatima, and their anger seemed much more focused on the Bamiyan shelter director, Najeeba, and of course on Zakia above all.

Shmuley called me that night, and he was ebullient. He had just attended a genocide conference in Kigali with President Kagame, and the Rwandan president was on board with Shmuley's African rescue plan. I thought he had already been on board, but now he was apparently really on board. "Our donor, she wants to educate them, give them jobs, bring them to the United States," Shmuley said. "We have the support of the State Department, we have everything ready to go, we just need passports. Samantha Power assured me she was interested in helping them, sympathized with their plight, and she would try to get their team on board. I took her assurances to heart." The American donor, a high-net-worth individual, would pay the costs of getting Zakia and Ali to Rwanda and give them a stipend for their living expenses; President Kagame would treat them as his personal guests.

Shmuley's enthusiasm was infectious, and he did have the attention of the State Department, although I'm not sure how deep their support for his plan really went. It was deep enough, though, to energize the American embassy to reach out to Ali and Zakia through an Afghan employee, Zmaryalai Farahi. After a chat on the telephone, he told them they would have to come into the embassy to discuss it further in person. When Ali tried to visit the American embassy, however, he only got as far as Massoud Circle in Wazir Akbar Khan before he saw that they would have to pass two or three cordons of Afghan police and guards just to get to the beginning of the road leading to the embassy. Suspicious that it was a setup to get them arrested, Ali turned away and stopped answering Zmaryalai's calls.

Around the same time, Aimal Yaqubi had started calling Ali aggressively, as Ali recalled it, ordering Ali to meet with him to pick up the thousand dollars he was delivering from Shmuley. The fixer's pushiness frightened the couple, and Ali just stopped picking up when he called. Ali was now no longer talking to the two contacts who perhaps could help them to safety, and he was only barely speaking to Jawad and me.

Shmuley was mystified. At my suggestion he had offered Aimal a bonus if he was able to help the couple get out of the country, but the amount was much more than I expected: $5,000. Perhaps that was the problem. In a society where two hundred dollars a month is a living wage, five grand is a lot of money. Even compared to Aimal's fees as a fixer, two hundred dollars a day, five grand was just too much incentive. In a way it was a small metaphor for the entire failed American enterprise in Afghanistan: Throwing money at the problem, however well intentioned, often makes matters worse.

Examples of this phenomenon abound. Consider a $35 million "go fly a rule-of-law kite" program, dreamed up and funded by a United States Agency for International Development (USAID) contractor, a commercial firm that is now known as Tetra Tech DPK.[20] Their idea was to stage a public event at which they would hand out kites, comic books, and posters with slogans printed on them touting equal rights for women and respect for the rule of law. Hundreds of kids and some adults showed up. Because the contractor was an American company, a large contingent of police was on hand to protect the American employees. First, no one could read the slogans on the kites and posters, let alone the text-heavy comic books; most of the kids were too young, and most of the adults who came were either jobless or policemen—neither a group with a high literacy rate.[21] Then handing out the kites went badly awry when policemen systematically stole them from the kids who had come, in order to take them home to their own cildren, beating some of the kids at the event with sticks when they didn't cooperate. Finally, gender equality was hard to come by. The few times any girls got their hands on the free kites, their fathers took them away and gave them to their sons instead. Despite critical coverage[22] that made the fly-a-kite program a laughingstock in the aid community, the contractor deemed it such a success that it was repeated later in Herat, and the contractor continued to dream up other methods of public outreach funded by U.S. taxpayers' money.

Similarly, indiscriminate American largesse dispensed by the embassy financed a rock concert in a country where rock music is little followed, infuriating the mullahs; a yoga charity with the stated goal of getting the Taliban to the peace table via the yoga mat; an Afghan adaptation of *Sesame Street*[23] for Tolo TV, featuring the American ambassador posing in Kabul with Grover, in all likelihood a war-zone first.[24] The American embassy also pumped more than $100 million into underwriting indigenous television stations, so that any minor press conference in Kabul has more television cameras[25] in attendance than most major news events in New York City or Washington, D.C. None of this was any more sustainable long-term than flying a kite; all will come crashing down once the American-financed windfall ends.

That May when we dialed Ali's number, we got love-song ringtones, a different one every few days, but he never answered. One frequent song was "Your Unkempt Hair," by the famous Afghan singer Ahmad Zahir.

Afghan women are rarely seen in public without at least a head scarf.

> *If the early morning breeze*
> *Should ruffle your unruly hair*
> *All hearts would be ensnared*
> *In that trap of love and suffering.*[26]

∽§∾

# 7

# HONOR HUNTERS

The lovers had no idea how many friends they had, but late that May and early June it was hard to persuade them that they had any. Everything seemed to be going wrong for them. Zakia's family was actively looking for them. They were miserable in hiding. Escape abroad seemed impossible. Money was running out. Faced as the couple was with a hopeless situation, their suspicious refusals to accept aid made it all worse.

While their hideout at Ali's aunt's house on the hill in Chindawul seemed secure, it was crowded and small and a hard place for anyone to spend much time. Remaining in hiding was getting increasingly difficult, particularly for Ali, but if either of them still wanted to flee abroad, they had a funny way of showing it. They were no longer answering the phone at all—not to Rabbi Shmuley's fixer, Aimal, not to the American embassy's human-rights officer, not even to us at the *New York Times*. They were low on prospects and almost out of hope.

Their pursuers had come to town in force, and Zakia's brothers and cousins were being spotted often. Zakia's father, Zaman, had left Bamiyan and resettled his immediate family in Kabul. This was partly because they had suffered so much contempt from their Hazara neighbors after they became the nationally notorious villains persecuting Zakia and Ali and partly because Zaman could not bear the humiliation of facing his Tajik neighbors after the loss of his honor. Mostly, though, as they told everyone who would listen, they wanted to exact revenge on the lovers, no matter what it took. Zaman and his sons had given up their tenancy on the farm in Bamiyan and looked for what work they could find as day laborers in Kabul, expecting to find the couple there.

"Honor and dishonor is like this: According to Islamic and shariah law, the girl cannot run away from home," explained Zakia's cousin Najibullah, an uneducated farm laborer. "It will be seen by the people as, 'Ha, your daughter has run away. You should no longer live in this village. If she had not run away, her father never would have quit the village. He quit it because he is so dishonored that he cannot live here anymore,'" he said. "All the people will mock him and jeer at him, like, 'If you were a man, why did your daughter run away? Why didn't you stop her?' They say these things, so we cannot let it be. He is her father, and I am her uncle's son, but it hurts our honor, too. I cannot live in Bamiyan any longer myself when they say my uncle's daughter ran away. We could not bring her back, so people will say to us, 'If you were men, had daring and courage, why couldn't you get your daughter back from the government?'"

One of Zakia's other cousins, Mirajuddin, was sitting with Najibullah; the two young men were among the relatives left in Kham-e-Kalak, although they no longer farmed the land and would soon join Zaman and his sons in Kabul to hunt the couple down. They had been in the courtroom when the melee broke out, although Zakia says they were not among those family members who attacked her physically. They were not close enough blood relatives to feel entitled to rip her clothes off and touch her, even if violently. "Your life is your honor, like your wife is your honor, and if your honor leaves you and goes to someone else, then this life is worthless," Mirajuddin said. "If someone takes your wife, your life is not worth living." Their position reflected a broader societal concern, as the cousins saw it. "If today the government doesn't do something about this, then tomorrow the wife of a farmer will elope with a schoolboy or a businessman and will say she can't live with her husband. So in this way, after the first one left, the others will follow." Zakia, in short, had challenged the entire structure of Afghan patriarchal society, and if she was not stopped, all women would abandon the husbands chosen for them. ("First one wants freedom, / Then the whole damn world wants freedom," as the late Gil Scott-Heron put it in his song "B Movie.")

In fact, there is a lot at stake for the women's-rights movement in Afghanistan, even far beyond its borders. Afghanistan, because of the involvement of the West since 2001, is the only such country where serious efforts are under way to improve the lot of its women. "Afghanistan is still the great battleground of women's rights in the twenty-first century," says Nasrine Gross, an Afghan sociologist and women's advocate. If women could win some measure of gender equality and equal treatment before the law in a country as backward and abusive as Afghanistan, that would be a provocative example to disenfranchised women in those other countries, such as Saudi Arabia and Somalia, Pakistan and Yemen, the Gulf satrapies and Iran. "There are some countries that are very powerful in certain ways, and women's rights is not something they want to discuss," Ms. Gross says. By "certain ways," she means power that comes from possessing vast oil and gas wealth. "They use the lack of women's rights as a means of controlling their own countries, and they want to keep Afghanistan at bay in terms of women's rights so Afghanistan will not become a role model for their societies. A place so poor, so illiterate, so backward, they cannot stand it if this poor Afghanistan would be a model of women's rights."[1]

Internally Afghanistan has long been a battleground for women's rights, but the battle is one that women and their advocates have always lost. Probably in no other country[2] have so many rulers been toppled over this particular issue, going back to King Habibullah, who opened the earliest girls' schools and ushered in some rights for women before he was assassinated in 1919. His son,

King Amanullah Khan, went much further, banning the veil for women, instituting girls' education in rural areas, and outlawing polygamy. King Amanullah began his reign as a popular leader, credited with defeating the British in the Third Anglo-Afghan War. When he returned from a visit to Europe with his liberal-minded queen, Soraya Tarzi, he declared at a public event that Islam did not require women to be covered, whereupon Queen Tarzi tore off her veil and the other government wives present did so as well. Under his rule women were allowed to divorce and to choose their husbands, bride prices were outlawed, women were encouraged to work and study. But in a country with no roads and little infrastructure of any kind and a weak central government and bureaucracy, Amanullah was unable to persuade his countrymen to embrace his reforms and instead provoked an uprising of mullahs and conservatives that drove him from power in 1929.[3]

This uprising was fueled in part by British agents, whose country was eager to get back at King Amanullah for its recent humiliation. They circulated pictures showing Queen Tarzi wearing a sleeveless gown at a state function and allowing her hand to be kissed during the European tour. Even today most educated women will not shake hands with men, while bare shoulders and arms in public would provoke a riot in Kabul.

Amanullah's successor, Nadir Shah, tried to institute reforms but was himself assassinated. Subsequent Afghan rulers were much more cautious about women's-rights issues. Not until the Communist era in the 1970s was any successful effort made to extend rights to women, and the sweeping progress decreed by the Communists on gender equality was the major reason for the uprising against them by mujahideen and their followers.[4] Their problem was with feminism, not with Communism. Their jihad was first of all against women's rights, and later against schools for girls, the right to divorce, and women in the workplace and public life. They did not object to Communism as an economic or political system; it was equal rights for women that bothered them.[5] When many of these mujahideen leaders later joined with the Americans to oust the Taliban, the alliance was not motivated by the Taliban's social policies; in most cases Afghan warlords were as hard-line on women's issues as the Taliban, and often even more regressive. The Taliban at least outlawed *baad,* and they officially disapproved of honor killings not based on their own judicial processes.[6]

The concept of honor and killing women to uphold that honor is not unique to Afghanistan. In ancient Rome the paterfamilias or dominant male within a household had a legal right to kill a sister or a daughter who had extramarital sex or a wife who committed adultery.[7] Othello's murder of Desdemona was an honor killing and typical of honor killings in that the woman is given no real recourse to plead her case; the victim's guilt or innocence becomes subordinate to the man's sense of the violation of his honor. This goes some way to explaining the murder of rape victims by their own families in Afghanistan.

The eminent anthropologist Thomas Barfield[8] of Boston University, who is president of the American Institute of Afghanistan Studies, says there is a sort of blood-feud belt, where honor killings of women were historically endemic, that stretches from Spain throughout the Mediterranean basin, across the Middle East, Arabia, Iran, and Afghanistan and then ends in Pakistan. East of that, north of that, south of it—in China or Mongolia, Southeast Asia or sub-Saharan Africa, Northern Europe or Russia—the concept of honor killing is pathological and rare, rather than socially acceptable and widespread.

With the notable exception of Saudi Arabia,[9] however, most modern societies, including Islamic societies, in the honor-killing belt have successfully criminalized the practice, just as nearly all societies have moved away from the concept of men's ownership of women. Even Ayatollah Ali Khamenei in fundamentalist Iran has condemned the practice of honor killing, and as with most Islamic scholars, Sunni and Shia, he insists that honor killing has no theological basis in Islam.[10]

A weak central government throughout Afghanistan's modern history, three and a half decades of war, and low levels of education and literacy[11] have helped to sustain abusive customary practices like honor killings.[12] "Dealing with the status of women has brought down more regimes in Afghanistan than anything else," Professor Barfield says. Both King Amanullah's premature reforms and the Communists' excessively ambitious efforts provoked a strong backlash, contributed to prolonging abusive customs, and made most modern leaders unwilling to confront conservatives on such controversial issues. Even today women's groups that protest honor killings typically refrain from challenging the concept underlying them, that women are the property of men, who are in absolute control of regulating their behavior.

In that ancient honor belt, Afghanistan has been a major holdout.[13] "The state in Afghanistan has not been able to move its writ into family affairs. The Afghans feel that is not a state responsibility," Professor Barfield says. Other states throughout that belt developed strong ruling systems where the state could and did inject itself into family and social affairs. "The state in the rest of the world has moved its power all the way down to the family level, but in Afghanistan, even today, the state is very hesitant to regulate family affairs. If there's a revenge killing, because it's murder, when it's brought to their attention, they will act, but on the other hand if it doesn't come to the state's attention, they don't look for it."

Given the attitudes of Zakia's family, she and Ali were doing their best to stay hidden, but in the crowded little house on the side of the Chindawul Hill, Ali was increasingly irritable. With the aunt and her children, as many as eight people were sharing perhaps four hundred square feet and a tiny yard. Every food purchase, every bucket of water, involved an exhausting climb up the steep hill. Complicating matters for them, Zakia was not feeling well and was constantly complaining of stomach cramps and pains and nausea—dysentery is rampant in a city that long ago outgrew what primitive sewage system it had. She did not suffer as much from the inability to go out, but she sensed that Ali's aunt resented her presence there and did not approve of her marriage to Ali. The aunt tolerated them because her brother Anwar had asked her to do so. Zakia was also lonely. She still missed her mother and father and brothers and sisters, the populous household in which she had spent her entire life, however much they wanted to kill her. She especially missed Razak, her lively nine-year-old brother, the much-doted-upon youngest male of the family. "I love him so much," she told Ali. "It's hard to think I will never see him again."

Zakia and Ali began arguing with each other over little things, and Ali was confused and defensive. This was not what he had expected their life together would be like. The long days of hiding at home were uncomfortable, but when Ali went out, Zakia worried constantly that her family or the police would find him. Suddenly one day, impulsively, he decided to rejoin the army. He had one year left on his enlistment, and he could go back without any real penalty as a deserter. Zakia was against it, and they argued, but she eventually agreed.

"I couldn't stay jobless forever," he said. "I have to do something to make back that money that we borrowed from people. They will not let us keep their money forever, one day they will ask for it." He'd had two months of freedom with his wife, and now it was time to work, as he put it. But the two-hundred- to two-hundred-fifty-dollar monthly army salary was not going to make much of a dent in their debts. There was a more practical reason to reenlist: Once in the military, stationed on a base, he would be virtually immune from arrest by the police. "I was going out a lot, and it wasn't good for me—it was dangerous—and I thought, why not join the army and be safe, plus make money?" He had managed, through the uncle of one of his sisters' husbands, to be allowed to rejoin as a bodyguard to a Hazara commander in the Afghan National Army. The commander was stationed at the Kabul International Airport, so Ali would not be far away from Zakia and could visit her on weekends. Even the uniform would help him to hide, although it meant that all his long black hair would be shorn to a military close-crop. The haircut proved to be not a bad disguise. One day when he was heading home on weekend leave to see Zakia, he passed right by his father-in-law, completely unnoticed by Zaman.

During this time we had begun talking with Ali and Zakia

again, and we decided that it was time to engage with them about
the Rwanda option that Shmuley had put on the table. It seemed
like they were never going to deal with Aimal Yaqubi directly,
and Shmuley was insistent that we offer them this opportunity.
It put me in an awkward position, but I didn't feel right letting
them pass it up for lack of the right messenger. We got Ali and
Zakia to sit down with Anwar, Jawad, and me, to talk it through.
Again we explained what they could expect in Africa, a minimum of six months of isolation in Rwanda while they waited for
onward visas—and no guarantee of those, though chances would
be good. It was clear they had soured on the idea, but in any case
their lack of passports was a deal breaker. Zakia had a new *tazkera,*
or ID card, by then, but they were unwilling to risk going to the
passport office with criminal charges still lodged against them, and
without passports Rwanda was a nonstarter. Rabbi Shmuley was
disappointed, but not daunted. Within a few days, he called to say
that he was fed up and ready to make a move, and he wanted my
advice on what to do about Fatima Kazimi.

"We're friends, right?"

"Sure."

"So tell me the truth."

"Okay."

"Should we save Fatima?"

I stalled for a moment to collect my thoughts, realizing what he
probably had in mind. "Save her how?"

"Get her out, save her. Rwanda."

"Okay, I see. Can I get back to you on that?"

That June we were all getting frustrated and anxious for some
sort of action. Stasis served no one's interest, least of all that of
Zakia and Ali, who remained elusive and unpredictable even toward Jawad and me. The fixer Aimal Yaqubi and the American
embassy were having a still-harder time pinning down Ali. The
embassy began calling me to try to get him to pick up calls from
them, and Aimal called us to complain that he was getting nowhere. At one point Aimal accused us of using our influence with
the couple to obstruct his efforts. Aimal had five hundred dollars to

give them as a donation from Rabbi Shmuley's mystery benefactor, he said, and they still wouldn't cooperate (the amount had shrunk since we'd first heard about it).

Shmuley was more frustrated with this inaction than anyone. He related to me a long conversation he'd had with an embassy official, public-affairs officer Robert Hilton, about the case. "Here we have a story that encapsulates why we're there, a story that has fired the American imagination, and you guys are not even involved in helping. You left it to a bunch of laypeople like us who don't know what they're doing."

Mr. Hilton told him, as Shmuley explained, that the embassy had to consider the sensibilities of the host country, which only incensed him. "What about the sensibilities of American readers? What about the sensibilities of a hundred thousand troops there and the trillion dollars we spent, and you can't get a woman who's going to be killed out of the country? A fricking trillion dollars, I told him."

Hilton pointed out that there were criminal charges against the couple that would somehow have to be adjudicated, and the United States couldn't be seen to be circumventing Afghanistan's legal system, in which it had invested more than a billion dollars over the past decade.

"Are you telling me you're going to abide by a corrupt judge's order to send her back to her family to be killed or raped?" Shmuley in righteous mid-rant was a force to be reckoned with. "This is ridiculous. This story has crystallized for all of us why we're there. We're there to protect people like Zakia." He had her name down by now. "All we have to do is get this woman a passport."

Shmuley was livid after he recounted this conversation to me. "I don't think the embassy is going to be helpful, but one way or another we're going to get them out, and it's going to be a big story when we get them out, and the U.S. government had no role whatever," he said. "After a trillion dollars, we can't save a woman from an honor killing because we're worried about hurting someone's feelings in the government? The American government can't do it? The American government is afraid of the Afghan government? Let them be more afraid of the American public. What the hell are we doing there? What have we managed to change there? We can't have these people die and achieve zero. So now a couple of bozos in New Jersey are going to do what the U.S. government cannot do. They seem to be under strict orders: Let's tiptoe out of Afghanistan and make no waves."

This kind of accommodation is rampant in the waning days of the Western intervention in Afghanistan. The case of a girl named Gulnaz, who was forced to marry her rapist, is a good example. The European Union suppressed a film it had commissioned that featured her plight, concerned that it would embarrass the Afghan government. British-based filmmaker Clementine Malpas found Gulnaz, then only nineteen, in Kabul's female prison, Badam Bagh, where she had been held for more than a year, and featured her in the EU-financed documentary on women in Afghanistan, which she called *In-Justice*. In the film, Ms. Malpas related how Gulnaz had been given a three-year prison sentence after she was raped by a cousin, Assadullah Sher Mohammad; Gulnaz gave birth to their child while in prison. When she appealed the case, her sentence was increased to twelve years,[14] but an Afghan judge offered her freedom if she would marry her rapist.

When officials at the EU mission in Kabul saw the film, they decided to withhold it from release, threatening the filmmaker with legal action if she allowed it to be aired. Ostensibly the reason was to protect the women in the film, Gulnaz as well as two other victims, from retribution. The EU rejected the position taken by the filmmaker that Gulnaz and the others in the film had given informed consent. It was a surrender by EU diplomats to Afghan cultural sensitivities. That was confirmed when the *New York Times* reported that e-mails from the EU's attaché for rule of law and human rights, Zoe Leffler, had told the filmmaker that the EU "has to consider its relations with the justice institutions in connection with the other work that it is doing in the sector."

In the ensuing furor, President Hamid Karzai ordered the girl released from prison—but made it clear that he expected her to marry her rapist as the court had ordered, according to the *Times*[15] account by Alissa J. Rubin.

"Gulnaz said, 'My rapist has destroyed my future,'" Ms. Malpas said, recounting their conversation. "'No one will marry me after what he has done to me. So I must marry my rapist for my child's sake. I don't want people to call her a bastard and abuse my brothers. My brothers won't have honor in our society until he marries me.'"

Women's groups objected and lobbied to have Gulnaz given refuge in a shelter. Then the news moved on and everyone lost interest in the case; the documentary was never officially released— another fifty thousand euros down the EU drain, part of some 18.2 million euros the EU spends annually on gender-focus programs,[16] not counting bilateral donor money from its member nations.

By 2014 history was being rewritten in Gulnaz's case. Mary Akrami, the head of an organization called the Afghan Women Skills Development Center, who says she was the first to open a women's shelter in Afghanistan (reportedly financed by the UN Women organization, as with the shelter in Bamiyan), claims that the international press and particularly Gulnaz's lawyer, Kimberley Motley (who took on the case after the documentary controversy erupted), deliberately distorted what had happened to Gulnaz. "The court married her by her consent," Ms. Akrami said. "She was not raped, but in fact she loved the guy and had a love affair with him. She then agreed to marry him. Her family reconciled with the man's family. They live together now and are happy. They have a child and are living in Kabul."

That is not how Kim Motley sees it, and she had visited Gulnaz as recently as mid-2014. The young woman, now twenty-two or twenty-three years old, really is married to her former rapist and does not deny that is what he is. He treats her decently, she told Ms. Motley, does not beat her, and provides for her and their daughter. Kim said that after the controversy over the documentary erupted, she at one point had offers from a dozen Western countries to provide Gulnaz with asylum. At the time Gulnaz was staying in Mary Akrami's shelter. "The minister of women's affairs and the shelter were blocking me from taking her to get a passport," she said. They saw reconciling with and marrying her rapist as the only solution that was in her interest, and history just had to be rewritten to make that possible, Ms. Motley said. "She never once denied to me that her cousin was her rapist; she was fifteen when it happened. She was even tied up when she was raped. There was never any ambiguity about that. She did finally marry him, but that's because the only way she could leave that fucking shelter was if she married this guy."

The sorts of offers of asylum that Gulnaz initially got had dried up by 2014, as more Afghan women saw flight from the country as their only salvation, and Western countries began to worry that granting asylum in such cases would undermine their efforts to promote women's rights within the country.

It was that attitude that had made an embassy rescue for Zakia and Ali increasingly unlikely, and all the more difficult for a couple with a criminal case against them. The conundrum raised by the criminal charges incensed Rabbi Shmuley. "That's the biggest farce of all. You fall in love with someone and it's a criminal case? I hope you will write something about these God-only-knows-how-many dead Americans and a trillion dollars in treasure so our government can respect a barbaric government. This is called the rule of law? I don't even know how they can say that with a straight face. Shaming them in the media is the only thing that's going to work. These people have to live like rats. Let's get them out."

Still, he couldn't get Ali and Zakia out when they had no passports—nor any legal way to secure them. But he could save someone else—and his mystery benefactor was willing to finance it, the government of Rwanda was willing to make it happen, and, he said, they were ready. They would save Fatima Kazimi. Just one thing bothered him about that. So, he wanted me to tell him frankly, did Fatima Kazimi really have grounds to fear for her life? "I'm worried that maybe she's just taking advantage of the situation and is now attempting to use this to get out of Afghanistan when we're trying to focus on Zakia and Ali, who seem to be in far greater danger." Yes, that sounded like Fatima all right, but I said nothing aloud. Answering him would put me in an ethically difficult position. If I had given him my unadorned, honest opinion, I would have said, *No, I really don't think she is in danger.* If that ruined the chance Shmuley was handing her to escape Afghanistan, what if she really was in danger? What right did I have to determine her fate and probably that of her family by expressing my opinion, particularly if I was wrong? I would get back to him, was the most I could say, and that was still kind of damning.

Up in Bamiyan even Fatima's allies were dismissive of any danger to her life. "There isn't any threat against her from other people, against her or her family. We would not let that happen," said the Bamiyan police chief, General Khudayar Qudsi. When the attorney general's office tried to interrogate her, he said, the police intervened to block it. "There was no basis, so we will not recognize such an action. The provincial attorney general based their request on accusations of Zakia's family, but there was no proof of Fatima Kazimi's involvement in the shelter escape," Chief Qudsi said. As for risks to her from Zakia's family? "It's not true. She has her own personal bodyguards who will take care of her safety, police bodyguards. That is our job and our responsibility. I think it's just an excuse so she can leave the country."

It seemed clear that what Fatima Kazimi wanted, like many Afghans, was a better life, and she had despaired of ever finding one in Afghanistan. That, however, does not qualify as "a well-founded fear of persecution" or any of the other generally accepted grounds for granting asylum or refugee status.

I felt like I had no choice but to share this view with Shmuley. My reporting had made her out to be one of the heroes of the piece, and he was about to reward her for it. Before I could reach Shmuley, though, Fatima called to say she was leaving that day for India, where she would be picking up her Rwandan visa. She had just the night before tried to leave through Kabul International Airport with a visa from the Rwandan government issued online, but Afghan airline officials had never seen an e-visa before and turned her away.

Shmuley had moved quickly. I called him back later that day, and he was in a celebratory mood. "Fatima arrived in Delhi. She's out of Afghanistan, thank God, and I hope we gave them security. They're on their way to Rwanda. Thank you for everything."

I told him I had belatedly come to the conclusion she was scamming everyone. Looking back, I figured she had probably planned this from the day of that first e-mail.

"We feel a sense of satisfaction," Shmuley said. "We got her out of there, thank God. Some people may not believe they are in danger, but we did the right thing." Shmuley reminded me a bit of the photographer Diego when he'd just found a beam of light coming through the ceiling and couldn't hear anything else anyone said.

In addition to the right to settle in Rwanda—and quite possibly becoming the first Afghans there in history—Fatima and her husband and four children would be given housing by President Kagame, and Rabbi Shmuley's benefactor was going to provide them with a twenty-thousand-dollar stipend to live on for the year, more than adequate for Rwanda. "We want to avoid an unhealthy dependency," he said.

He was finally ready to tell me who the benefactor was. "She is prepared to be named, with one caveat: so long as it does not endanger the couple." It was Miriam Adelson, the wife of casino magnate and multibillionaire Sheldon Adelson.

Ms. Adelson did not want credit as a Jewish person for saving a Muslim couple from their backward society. She was just moved by their case and wanted to help them, and anyone affected by their story as well. There was no other agenda here; Miriam's motives were purely humanitarian, he said. "The real hero of the story is not me, it was Miriam Adelson, who got me interested in their case. After a while, I became personally involved. I now really cared which direction this was going."

Fatima spent a couple of days in India, which coincided with a gala that Rabbi Shmuley's World Values Network put on in New Jersey with a variety of A-list celebrities and politicians, including Sean Penn, Governor Rick Perry of Texas, Governor Chris Christie of New Jersey, and Elie Wiesel.[17] Shmuley's aides organized a video hookup to New Delhi so Fatima could thank Miriam and President Kagame for rescuing her. Miriam might have had no particular agenda, but Paul Kagame did. Once seen as a hero in the West for pulling his country through the Rwandan genocide, Mr.

Kagame was lately in need of some good press, having been accused of murdering opponents, stifling dissent, and turning Rwanda, once Africa's bright black hope, into an autocratic state run by yet another African Big Man.[18] Like Shmuley, Miriam Adelson was a staunch supporter and defender of Israel, and Israel in turn was a staunch ally of Rwanda. The two countries' backers would see the shared experience of genocide as their bond; their critics would see governments with similarly appalling human-rights records fighting against a growing status as pariah states, despite their ennobling pasts.

The next day Fatima and her family were on the long flights from Delhi to Dubai and Dubai to Kigali.

The next time we spoke to Ali, in this case by phone, we told him that Fatima had escaped to Africa, after telling the people who wanted to help him that she, too, needed to be saved. He was astonished.

"Fatima went to Africa?" He laughed for a couple of minutes, then regained his composure. It was, he said, one more reason not to consider Africa as a way out. He and Zakia didn't want to be someplace where the only other person in the country who spoke their language was Fatima Kazimi.

His vehemence surprised me, and I asked why he felt that way. "She didn't help us at all," he said. "She didn't help me, she didn't help Zakia escape, she didn't do anything for us. One day we will run into each other and talk." It was an emotional outburst.

I said it was pretty undeniable that Fatima had prevented Zakia's family from taking her out of court that day and probably killing her. "That was all she did, and I respect that, but besides that she didn't do anything for us." That was underselling Fatima quite a bit, whether or not she had used the couple's situation to her own benefit. I didn't understand his attitude and would not for some time to come.

# 8

~ىۈ~

# THE IRRECONCILABLES

Hope is not much of a plan, but it was about the only plan they had. "This world is sprung with our hopes, the past is built on our hopes, you spend your life with hopes," Ali said in his dreamy way on one of the few times in May when we were able to reach him, "and I'm just hoping now that God will help us." When Ali did choose to answer his phone, either he would barely listen to us or he would suddenly appeal to us to make the couple's decisions for them. The worst thing was that Ali was unwilling to come down to earth and get serious about their safety. Given the number of sightings of Zakia's male relatives not far from the Chindawul area of Kabul where the couple was hiding with his aunt, it was clear that place was no longer safe. Since the aunt was Anwar's sister, it wouldn't be hard for Zakia's family to find out where she lived, at least the general area, and then stake it out until Ali or Zakia came along. That might well have been what was already happening with the near misses. Ali always agreed with us when we lectured him about this, but we could have been talking to a wall.

One day Jawad and I sat down and wrote out a list of talking points for the next time we had Ali on the telephone and he was in half a mood to listen or if we were able to meet with him when he was on leave from his army post:

- They can't just stay in hiding forever. Sooner or later they will be caught. That's what everyone who works on these family disputes says.
- If they're caught, they'll both be taken to jail. That could well mean that Zakia would be sexually abused in custody, which happens routinely. Jail for a woman is much worse than a shelter, which is at least run by other women.
- They should think about at least talking to the people who run the Women for Afghan Women shelter. They don't have to do what they say, just hear them out.
- The WAW lawyers are very good, and recently they won a case similar to Zakia and Ali's, and while the case was in court, the woman had to stay in their shelter for only a month.
- The lawyers say their case is a strong one and they're certain they can prevail legally. They cannot do that, however, unless Zakia is no longer a fugitive and is somewhere so they can produce her in court. She could come into the shelter while Ali can stay in hiding.
- The head of WAW, Manizha Naderi, is happy to talk to Ali, and although she is in the United States now, she will call him in the evening, and this is the number she will be calling from.
- The WAW shelter is nothing like the one in Bamiyan. If they decide to go to the shelter to discuss their case with the lawyers there, we can go with them and guarantee that they can leave if they want to do so.
- If they ever change their minds and decide to leave Afghanistan, they're going to need to have passports, and they're not going to be able to get them safely while there are criminal charges against them. They need to get the legal case settled. The only countries they could go to without passports are Iran, which is dangerous, and Pakistan, which is difficult.

We drilled away on these talking points every time Jawad got Ali on the phone, and with his father and brothers as well, but he would not even agree to go to the shelter and hear what the lawyers said, let alone agree to Zakia's checking into the shelter so their case could go to court. When we spoke to Zakia, she deferred to Ali.

A week or more went by with no answer, just an out-of-service message on his number, and then finally came one of the familiar ringtones, from the blind Iranian singer Moein and his song "Past":

> *Have no grief about the past,*
> *For the past has passed.*
> *Grief can never remake the past.*
> *Think of the future, of life, of joy.*
> *And if thirst should find no river,*
> *Just drink one drop, and be satisfied.*[1]

This time Jawad made some headway, and Ali agreed to meet with us that Friday; his commander had given him a three-day leave. "He was scared," Jawad said. "I told him, 'Look, we haven't done anything to you. We've been to your house, been to your father, we could have turned you in anytime. You just have to trust us.'"

"Even today I didn't tell my wife I was going to see you, because she might have said no," Ali said. "The last time you came to see us"—when Zakia's brother was spotted near the Pamir Cinema—". . . well, she's very nervous about me. She doesn't want me to go out at all. She thinks I'll be arrested, so she'll be in big trouble."

Again, we suggested, all the more reason to consider the shelter for her until their legal case was finished. Manizha Naderi of WAW had offered to make that more palatable for Ali by giving him a job as a security guard at the shelter, guarding the outside wall; he would not be allowed inside, since the shelters were female-only spaces, but he'd know Zakia was safe, and they could have chaperoned meetings from time to time. Nothing persuaded him.

"My wife said she cannot be there for even one day. She cannot be separated from me even one day," he said. I wondered if that was his wife speaking or him.

Manizha and her top lawyer at the time, Shukria Khaliqi, came up with a solution. Shukria found a way to take the couple's case to court without having Zakia stay in the shelter. "All they have to do is give us permission to take on the case," Manizha said. "Both of them would just need to meet Shukria. Shukria can go to wherever they say and take their testimonies. Then, after the case goes to the judge, Zakia would have to come to court to testify on her own behalf. I am really worried that they will somehow be caught by the police." If they were, it would be too late for Zakia to opt for placement in the shelter; women can voluntarily stay in shelters while their criminal cases are adjudicated, but only if they come in on their own. Once they're arrested, they are jailed until their court date.

Driven by a need for more money, Ali finally agreed to meet with Shukria, although without Zakia. They were broke again, and they could receive the donors' money from WAW only in person, so that WAW's accountants could verify that the right people had gotten it. In a society where corruption is the norm, people have to go to extremes to prove that their actions aren't dishonest. Ali repeatedly asked us to pick up the money for him. It just wasn't right for us to put ourselves in the middle of that, and besides, we wanted to get him in to meet WAW's capable lawyers.

Tough and articulate, Shukria is somewhat overbearing, and immediately on meeting him she dominated Ali, insisting he put his trust in her.

"I'll resolve this case in a month," she told him. "I'll work on this case until I find success. I'll get my contacts in the Ministry of Interior to put pressure on the elders up there, and I'll do it in complete confidence—I won't even register the case, so even my staff won't know about it." Ali, on the sofa near her desk, leaned away from her as she spoke, seeming to diminish physically under her peroration.

Then the accountant came in to hand over a thousand dollars to him from the donations WAW had received, following a ritual often used when an illiterate person is involved in a formal transaction. The accountant read out loud a document saying that Ali confirmed receiving the payment. Ali verbally confirmed that he understood that, put his inked thumbprint to the document, and exchanged the document for the money; during the transaction an aide videotaped every step.

Afterward Ali was buoyed. "As long as they do not ask to remove Zakia from me again, it's okay, they can take the case," he said. "Whoever defends the truth, I am ready to serve them." He was in such a good mood that he agreed to arrange for us to talk to Zakia in person and to bring her to Shukria so she could formally agree to be represented by WAW.

Ali perked up even more when he heard that Jawad had received a call from one of the elders from Kham-e-Kalak, Zakia's village, and the elder wanted to come and talk to us about their case. The elder had an idea that the *New York Times* was some sort of NGO and thought we might be able to act as intermediaries between Zakia's family and the couple. His name was Abdul Rab Rastagar, and Jawad and I arranged to meet him at the Herat Restaurant in Shar-e-Naw, downtown Kabul. It was large and always crowded and very public, with the traditional raised eating platforms scattered among trees around a garden, but without privacy screening. Diners would leave their shoes under the platforms and sit cross-legged among mats and cushions. Eating on mats on the floor is the norm in Afghan homes; this was a refinement of that practice, probably originally designed to keep livestock away from the table. A peacock in full finery roamed the aisles between the platforms, trailing a six-foot-long tail array and squawking loudly. We went early and chose seats from which we could watch the front entrance, in case Mr. Rastagar came in heavy. We knew he had been in touch with Gula Khan. The last time Gula Khan had spoken to us on the phone, he'd sounded as angry at us as at his sister; apparently someone had been reading or relating to him *Times* articles on the case.

Mr. Rastagar arrived alone and looked harmless enough. He was an older man, in his fifties probably, but quite self-possessed; the term "elders," as Afghans apply it, can mean either very old men, revered for their antiquity, or somewhat older men of position, revered for their power. Mr. Rastagar was an example of personal advancement by virtue of massive foreign aid. For the first couple years after the Taliban fell, he worked for an organization called UN-Habitat, which carried out rural-development programs in Bamiyan. Then he went to work as a supervisor for the provincial juvenile-detention center, a government-run facility also financed by international donors. His lofty title gave him the position that Zakia's family was so impressed by and in turn had made them entrust to him the important mission of contacting the NGO known as the *New York Times,* which they believed was in touch with the couple. Later we learned that Mr. Rastagar was just a glorified guard, a shift supervisor.

When Mr. Rastagar took off his shoes, there were holes in the soles of his socks. He sat down cross-legged on the platform with us, dressed in a brown *shalwar kameez* and wearing the Afghan *pakol,* the flat felt cap common throughout the country. He got right to the point.

"No one is telling you the truth about this case," he said. "Mohammad Zaman had to leave everything and come here to Kabul to work like a common laborer because of this case. The truth is that the girl was betrayed by Ali's sister. She brought her out so Mohammad Ali could come and rape her. Then the sister went to her and said, 'Zakia, now your fiancé won't marry you.'" Mr. Rastagar meant the putative fiancé that Zaman had arranged for Zakia—one of his nephews. "You see, the sister wanted to marry Zakia's fiancé, and that's why she did all this. So she said, 'I'll marry him, and you can marry Mohammad Ali. But Zakia absolutely didn't want to be with Mohammad Ali. She was raped, and that's why they took her to the shelter. They did not let her father and mother visit her because she was regretting what happened and she wanted to come home."

Mr. Rastagar paused, making eye contact with an effort, to see how that was sinking in. "There's more."

"Really?"

"Yes, two of his other sisters, they're prostitutes. We all know they're prostitutes, and I'm sure it's their fault that this happened."

How did he know this?

"I worked with them at UN–Habitat," he said. "Of course they're prostitutes. They worked there for the foreigners."

As he did?

"Yes, but they were girls. Everyone in the village knew they were prostitutes. When a stranger came to the village, we all knew whose house they were going to."

This counternarrative was delivered with smooth assurance, as if it were the most obvious explanation possible and, once apprised of it, any listener would see the rightness of Zakia's father's cause.

I suggested that Zakia would not have climbed out of the Bamiyan shelter and eloped with Ali if he were her rapist.

"The government set up that escape," he said. "She didn't want to. She's in hiding. No one knows where she is. Or if she is with him in the mountains, okay, she is with him in the mountains, but she didn't want to be there. Honestly, the father has been oppressed in this case."

Zakia's father was the real victim of the entire story, he continued. "Now he's in Kabul almost as a beggar because he's lost everything, everything," he said. "He didn't take care of his children, especially his daughters. He didn't do well by them, it's true. I don't approve of the man for this. He shouldn't have let his daughter go into the fields for this affair to take place."

But you said it was a rape?

"Or rape. It couldn't have taken place if he didn't let his daughter go into the fields unchaperoned. I wanted to beat Zaman myself, I was so angry at him."

He was particularly worked up about the shelter, letting a girl run away like that. "The shelter must have helped her escape," he said. "I have twenty-five children under my charge, and why do *they* not escape? It is just not possible." It was easy to imagine Mr. Rastagar subduing a passel of small children.

Officials in Bamiyan had made everything worse by not listening to the old man Zaman and his sons and by throwing him out of their offices when he came to complain, which by all accounts he did often. "The governor said to Zaman, 'Don't talk to me anymore, or I'll put you in jail next,'" Mr. Rastagar said.

That had led to an unstable situation, a rent in the fabric of the social order that could have far-reaching consequences. "The outcomes are going to be bad. The husband will do something, the first husband"—the one he had earlier described as the fiancé—"he is armed now, and he would kill anyone in this. I saw the father, he wants to commit suicide. The father, Zaman, he is weak, a weak person, but he is saying he will kill himself or else he will go and join the Taliban and go to Ghorband"—a notorious, Taliban-controlled district athwart the highway between Kabul and Bamiyan—"and if he finds any Hazara on the road, he will kill them."

In other words, suicide and mayhem, the random execution of strangers of the wrong ethnicity—it's the sort of thing that follows naturally when two people are foolish enough to fall in love.

"I don't like this father. He didn't raise his kids right," Mr. Rastagar said. Now he seemed eager to establish his credentials as an honest broker. "He didn't send his kids to school, so they grew up blind, and when blind persons go out, they get into trouble."

How about five thousand dollars—would that be enough to make old man Zaman happy? Just asking theoretically.

"I will work as hard as possible to resolve this case." Mr. Rastagar ignored the sum.

Seven thousand?

"The father will not return to Bamiyan. There's nothing left for him. Everyone turned on him. We have an Afghan proverb: When you are in need, your friends become strangers."

Ten thousand?

"The outcomes now are going to be bad. The first husband will do something, and it will be something that no one will be able to undo."

Mr. Rastagar said he would talk to the father. He added that he knew that already the first husband had spent twenty thousand dollars as a result of the elopement, to pay the bride price for the bride he never laid eyes upon, the wedding party that never took place. He would talk to Zaman. He was meeting him that afternoon, in fact. We told him we would find someone who would be authorized to negotiate for the couple, something we could not do. Our questions were merely exploratory.

When we parted, his last comment was peculiar. "If they do really love each other, it's okay."

The meeting was a modestly encouraging development. However mean-spirited the narrative Mr. Rastagar was peddling, it was clear that he was ready to deal and was probably acting on behalf of Zakia's father. Piling on charges of prostitution and rape was only a way of raising the stakes and improving Zaman's bargaining position. For their part, Ali and Zakia were ecstatic at the prospect of a negotiated settlement with her family. Although they realized there was every possibility her family would take any settlement money and still try to kill them, nonetheless it would mean the criminal charges against them would be withdrawn, the law would no longer be looking for them, and they would be free to get their passports. Ali scoffed when he heard the amount of twenty thousand dollars. "That is ten lakhs of rupees," he said, meaning afghanis. "In our village the usual bride price is less than three lakhs. You could marry three wives for ten lakhs."

There was no question of Jawad and I getting involved in any real negotiations, so with the couple's approval we turned to WAW and Shukria. We told her that Rastagar had floated a twenty-thousand-dollar figure, and she just laughed. She would be surprised if the family would not settle for five thousand, which made possible a settlement within the range of what donors had already sent to the couple; we told her that there were donors as well who had pledged to make up a bride price if that was not enough.

We were in Shukria's office when she called Rastagar and began to talk with him about the case. She quickly took his measure and started barking orders at him. He would get Zakia's father and he would bring him to her office to discuss the case, she told him. No, not next week, but two days later, on Saturday, she said. He promised to do so. "Don't be late, I'm a busy person," she said.

"This is fantastic," Manizha Naderi said. "Don't worry about what the elder is saying now. They always do that. That's what the people were saying about my nephew—that he raped and then kidnapped her. This is really great news, actually. We might have a chance in resolving this story."

Manizha was referring to the case of her own nephew and his wife, which was strikingly similar to that of Ali and Zakia. That couple eloped against the wishes of her family, who opposed it not because of ethnic or religious differences but because of class differences. The girl was from a family of Sayeds, people who consider themselves direct descendants of the Prophet Mohammad, a sort of Islamic nobility, who tend to want their children to marry other Sayeds. After the couple eloped, the girl's family claimed that she had already been married to her first cousin, and they even produced a mullah and witnesses who claimed to have been present when her father (although not the girl herself) had tied the *neka* on her behalf; they produced a *neka* document as well. Manizha persuaded her nephew to bring the girl to the shelter, and she remained there while Shukria brought her case to court. She won it with a simple stratagem: She challenged the girl's family and their witnesses to produce a single image of the alleged wedding ceremony. Since nowadays nearly everyone with any means at all has a camera phone, videos and stills of wedding ceremonies are typically taken by many of those present. When none of them could produce such an image, the judge invalidated the family's *neka* and legalized the couple's own marriage. It was that case that made Shukria so confident she could win Ali and Zakia's case, since there were witnesses who could confirm that until they eloped, Zakia's father had claimed only that she had been engaged, not married—and had changed his story regarding which cousin had been her intended.

The good news about a possible reconciliation gave a welcome boost to Zakia and Ali just as the home front began to unravel. Relations with Ali's aunt had become tense, and not just because the apartment was overcrowded. "They feel in danger, too. Even we do," Ali said. "Until we negotiate and make a deal and come together, we feel in danger. It's even risky when you're together with your friends. Someone who is your friend can harm you worse than someone who doesn't even know you. He might not realize what he's telling someone about you. If he's close to you, he will be dangerous to you."

One day Ali called Jawad, deeply agitated. We had given him a letter, on *New York Times* letterhead in Dari and English, with a copy to both him and his wife, a "To Whom It May Concern" letter that asked whoever read it to please call our bureau in Kabul and included Jawad's and my phone numbers. My thinking was that if one or the other of the lovers fell into the hands of police, the evidence of some foreign interest in their case might possibly prevent the worst from happening to them—particularly to Zakia— and it might help alert us to their situation more quickly. Now Ali was calling from his military deployment to ask whether that letter would protect Zakia from arrest by the police if she went out alone and was stopped.

No, it wouldn't, we told him. The most we could hope for was that it might protect her from summary rape, and that was iffy— the great majority of policemen cannot read or write, so she would have to be lucky enough to encounter someone who was senior enough to be literate and savvy enough to care what foreigners might think. It was a long shot.

What was going on? we asked Ali. It turned out that he had been transferred to Bagram Air Base, the massive American military base a couple hours' drive from the capital. "My wife called me and complained about my aunt and her daughter-in-law, who are mistreating her. She was upset and asked me to send her back to Bamiyan. I thought my aunt was someone I could trust and expected she would give us refuge, but now it seems she has slapped me in the face and my wife cannot stay with her. I don't know what to do. Sometimes I think I should commit suicide."

The country was in a state of suspense over the bitterly disputed results of the April presidential election, and it was clear there would have to be a second, runoff election in June. As a result, Ali's unit had been activated in preparation for deployment somewhere in the provinces to protect polling places, hence the transfer to Bagram. There was no longer any question of leave days every weekend; now he and Zakia were reduced to talking by phone again, and his next leave would not be until after elections, many weeks away.

Matters came to a head in their hideout, and the aunt demanded that Zakia leave as soon as possible. Zakia had been feeling ill for several days and wanted Ali to take her to a hospital. Relations had soured with Ali's aunt to the point where the aunt would not take her, and Zakia could not hope to find her way there alone. Moving out would also require a man to escort her; social norms made it nearly impossible for her to find another place on her own, and anyway Ali had unwisely—but typically—taken most of their money with him.

Ali said he would try to get permission to leave the base, but the next day when we spoke to him, he was even more despondent. Turned down for a leave because of his unit's pending deployment, he had tried to get a guard on the perimeter to let him sneak off the base but had been rebuffed. He had called his father to come down from Bamiyan to take care of his wife, but Anwar would need a couple of days to travel, and Zakia was increasingly frantic about leaving.

"It's because of my bad luck that these things keep happening," Ali said, and he told Zakia on the phone that he would try to escape. In a more levelheaded moment, much later, he was more honest about himself. "You buy danger for yourself by the things you decide to do."

We pleaded with Ali not to try to escape from Bagram, saying it could only end badly. He might not have known that base well, but I did. The largest American base in the country, Bagram was heavily guarded, with patrols, high-tech monitors, trip wires, pressure sensors, video cameras, surveillance blimps, and fences within fences. The Afghan National Army billets were within the broader American perimeter. Not only would escape be nearly impossible, but Ali risked being shot if he tried it.

We offered instead to arrange to take Zakia somewhere safe

ourselves, perhaps to a guesthouse or to the home of a woman. I called an Afghan-American woman who lived outside Kabul with her Afghan family—educated, Westernized people who were sympathetic to Zakia and Ali's plight—and she agreed to put Zakia up until Ali could join her. Ali refused the offer flatly, and we argued about it; I asked him why he didn't trust us. "I trust you. I even trust your dogs," he said, which is a common expression, invoking Afghans' almost universal contempt for canines. "But Zakia would never agree to stay with someone she doesn't know." Meaning he would never agree to let her. We suggested that she go to the WAW shelter until he could join her, but he rejected that out of hand.

It was two days before we heard from him again; his phone had stopped answering, and we suspected, rightly, that he'd gone ahead with his escape plan. He and two friends had climbed the main fence, carrying a blanket to drape over the rolled concertina wire that lay on the other side of it. He was crawling over the wire when a patrol came along and caught him.

"They nearly shot me when they saw me in the wire," he said once we got him on the phone; he had been locked up in solitary confinement during those two days when we could not reach him. "I was given a hard time, accused of being a spy. They told me you haven't spent one month in the army and now you want to sneak away from the base?" Taliban infiltrators were a constant worry in the Afghan National Army.

In the coming week, he tried twice more to escape the base and was each time punished. "I told them if you stop me a hundred times, I will still try to escape."

Anwar reached Kabul several days later after a dangerous journey. Hazaras need to take great care on both of the two main highways connecting Kabul with the Bamiyan Valley, one through Wardak Province slightly to the south, and the other through Parwan to the north. Both roads have stretches that go through Taliban territory, and while the roads are normally under government control, the Taliban do occasionally manage to set up flying roadblocks, as they are called, and Hazaras often do not get through alive when that happens. Reports of roadblocks ahead forced him to turn back twice. Anwar was delayed, too, by the funeral of someone in their village; however urgent his son's and his daughter-in-law's entreaties might have been, funerals take precedence over nearly everything, and Anwar was an old man, inclined to the long view.

Once in Kabul, though, he calmed his sister down. She agreed to give them a few days to find another place to stay. I passed Anwar a little money to help with that—Ali was still in the army lockup, so he could not go to collect money from WAW—and the last thing we wanted to see was Zakia and her father-in-law wandering the streets of Kabul, inviting arrest.

Ali was calmer when he heard that his father had arrived, and he thought he would soon find a way to get off the base to join them. In the meantime he had a request. Once they moved Zakia out of his aunt's house, how about if we got WAW to give them all the money they had received, and he would buy a house in Kabul so they did not have to rent any longer? A few thousand dollars would, he thought, be enough for a smaller home.

"Ali," we said to him, "your wife is in hiding. The police are searching for you both. Zakia's family is looking to kill you. You're in jail on the base. And you want to buy a house?"

That day Jawad got a call from Anwar, who also thought fugitive homeownership was a dumb idea. Jawad had called Anwar before, usually through one of his sons, but the old man had never before called him, and he did so now with Bismillah's help. He wanted to thank us for all we had done for his son, and he wanted us to know that he thought his son was wrong and foolish to have spurned offers of help and rejoined the army. Unless they were able to make a deal with Zakia's family—and even if they did—the couple's only hope to really live in peace was to leave Afghanistan. Anwar also wanted to meet us in person; it turned out he had lugged down from Bamiyan a hand-woven felt rug, which he said was a thank-you gift for helping his son. It was probably worth a month's earnings, yet I had no choice but to accept it.

Ismatullah called as well. "Ali does not realize what he has to do," he said. "He is too young to understand what is good or bad for him. Tell him he needs to listen to you. He needs to go outside the country. His life is in danger." Jawad asked Ismatullah why he didn't tell his brother that himself. But Ali was not answering his phone to his older brother. "He is tired of listening to everyone tell him what he has to do," Ismatullah said.

Then, to our surprise, a few days later Ali was freed from the base lockup and even managed to get out of Bagram on a leave, determined to desert for good this time. When we met Ali in Kabul, Jawad and I spent most of the time trying to persuade him to find a better hiding place, one where we could visit them more safely than if they were sharing a house with an Afghan family. They needed to *not* stay with relatives; relatives provide a trail to them. In response Ali was his usual blend of nervously insecure and unreasonably cavalier. He was hopeful that the mediation that Shukria was running with Zakia's father was going to bear fruit; in addition, Ali's aunt's son, Shah Hussein, had been meeting with Zakia's brothers to talk about a deal. "Didn't it occur to you," we asked, "that her brothers might follow his aunt's son or figure out where he's living, find her, and then find the two of you?" Again he brushed that aside. We said we would be willing to get them a private house with a wall around it and a driveway, which would make it possible for us to drive off the street and not be noticed by neighbors when we made a rendezvous with them. We would pay the four hundred dollars a month it would cost. Finally Ali agreed, as he often did, just to get us off his back, but instead of moving to the sort of place we'd suggested, he moved out of the aunt's house in Chindawul and into another house a few hundred yards down the hill. It was only a hundred dollars a month, so he suggested we could give them the three-hundred-dollar-a-month savings over what we had proposed; we refused to pay any of it. We had an ally in Anwar, and Jawad set to work persuading the old man that moving again, away from Chindawul and into a secure house, would be a good option for them as well as for us. The last thing I wanted was to feel responsible for their capture.

Reconciliation was starting to look less likely, too. Shukria was having a hard time with Zaman and his sons and supporters.

Initially willing to talk, Zakia's father had become aggressive and uncooperative. He accused Shukria of hiding Zakia in the WAW shelter and demanded to be allowed to look for her there.

"That man used such bad language," she said. "It was unacceptable." Amid her shouting and his cursing, she drove him from her office and WAW's administrative compound. Something had happened to make Zakia's family less willing to negotiate a settlement, and we would soon find out what that was.

There were many times when I marveled at my growing involvement with this couple. The line between observer and actor had first been crossed when we helped them escape from the police pursuit in Yakawlang, but now, with each passing week, further compromises seemed easier to make than to refuse: helping them with their housing, giving them advice, trying to talk them out of situations that might prove disastrous, urging them toward a sensible course of action. That's the thing about stepping over the line; once you do, it's hard not to do it again. Having helped them get this far, how could I just stop? I knew that if I turned my back on this young and often foolish pair of lovers, it would only be a matter of time before the worst happened, and I would never be able to forgive myself. The more I did for them, however, the more they expected me to do; the more dependent they became, the more independent they wanted to seem; the more I did, the more I felt obliged to do. I felt like their personal Friar Laurence, in an increasingly compromised scenario.

It's not as if Zakia and Ali's case was particularly terrible. On the scale of horrendous abuses of women in Afghanistan, Zakia's situation, so far, did not rate very high. Consider Lal Bibi, the young woman who was abducted and raped by a pro-government militia commander, who then married her to escape prosecution; or Bibi Aisha, her nose and ear cut off by her Taliban husband; or Gul Meena, chopped up with an ax and left for dead—all were far worse cases.

There were some cases similar to Zakia's as well, such as that of

Amina, whose family gave the same sort of guarantees and assurances that Zakia's family promised her if she returned.[2] Then they
killed her on the way home from a shelter—exactly what Zakia
thought would happen to her if she left the shelter to return to her
family. Similarly, Siddiqa[3] was coaxed home and then stoned to
death with her intended by her neighbors and relatives. Even more
similar was the story of Khadija and Mohammad Hadi, who were
also from Bamiyan, also a Tajik and Hazara couple. When Khadija
was taken into custody, her lover's angry neighbors drove his entire
family out of Bamiyan and he lost touch with Khadija, until she
disappeared and lost touch with everyone.[4]

So while there are many worse cases, they are expressions of
the sort of fate that awaits Zakia and Ali if events were allowed to
follow their natural course. While things had not gotten as bad as
they could have, it was still possible that they would. Like it or not,
their story had become mine, and I could not turn my back on it
as I nearly had after that first encounter in February 2014. It had
become clear that no one was going to step in and rescue them,
whisking them away to safe lives in America or Sweden. I realized
I would have to start thinking seriously about getting them out of
Afghanistan myself. I had already stepped across the line; why not
follow the story to its inevitable conclusion? If they ended up dead,
I would always regret not having tried harder. In this effort I had
one supporter, Rabbi Shmuley. During one of our late-night talks,
he started in on me after he finished with the American government. "You're the only one who can make this happen. You have
to make sure this story has a happy ending, and a happy ending is
not living in a cave in Afghanistan."

# 9

◦⟨૭⟩◦

# BIRDS IN A CAGE

An Afghan woman alone is easily run to ground, and suddenly, one day in June, Zakia became that woman, her husband ripped away from her, his aunt ready to disown her, and the police actively searching the Chindawul area for her. Her family had finally caught up to the couple, capturing Ali and turning him over to the police. This all happened just days after Zakia had learned what everyone had begun to suspect: she was pregnant.

Gentle-spirited Jawad would later describe that day as the most stressful of his life. I'm not sure what was worse, being there in the middle of it, as Jawad was, or not being there at all, as I was. When the call came that Ali had been arrested, Jawad was enjoying his Friday off out of town, an hour away from Kabul, while I was in Doha, Qatar, working on a Taliban story. Jawad got the news in a call from Shah Hussein, Ali's cousin and the son of the aunt who took the couple in and then kicked them out; both Shah Hussein and Ali had been picked up by the police. It was about 1:00 P.M. when Jawad heard, and he raced back to Kabul, spending most of the next eight hours continuously on the telephone; all I could do was check in from time to time and nudge matters along. "I must have made fifty phone calls that day and gotten another fifty," Jawad said; he had phones on two of the country's cell-phone networks, and he kept them both going, along with the bureau landline. The first call he made was to Anwar, who was with Zakia at their new home when the arrest happened. Shah Hussein had already called them with the news, and both of them were in tears. "Can you solve this for us, please?" Zakia asked Jawad.

Jawad called me in Qatar, and said, "What should I tell them?" I asked him where Ali had been taken. It was to the headquarters of Police District 1, and he had been arrested not far from where Zakia, Anwar, and he were staying in Chindawul, among the squatter dwellings that every year creep farther up the side of the steep little mountain above the Pamir Cinema. Surely if the police caught him near the Pamir, it would only be a matter of time before they canvassed the hillside neighborhood and found Zakia as well. For Ali it was just an arrest and possibly some jail time; for Zakia it was quite possibly the end of life as she knew it, with disgrace and defilement waiting for her in a police cell and the real possibility that the police would then hand her over to her family, which would be the end of her life, full stop.

"There's only one thing to do. Tell them they both need to get as far away from there as possible, and they should split up and go different ways." Jawad relayed the message.


Ali had thought his cousin Shah Hussein would be his guarantee of safety, and they stayed friendly after he and Zakia moved to the new house and away from the aunt. Shah Hussein often visited them, partly out of friendship, partly as protection. He was a senior noncom in the Afghan National Army and very much the older brother to his cousin, seven years his junior, and he tried to rein him in. Ali had started going out frequently, to visit friends or just to get air, and it was driving everyone in the family crazy, most of all Zakia. Shah Hussein had taken her side and tried to lay down the law.

"Don't leave the house," Shah Hussein told Ali. "If I come back

and find you are out, I'm going to shackle you to the furniture."
He was in the military police and produced a set of handcuffs to
back up the threat.

But that day, June 6, 2014, Shah Hussein was on leave and suggested that he and Ali go together to a wedding. Zakia said she was
okay with that, that as a man he could not be cooped up indoors all
the time. She had a house to keep, food to cook, laundry to do—
the men had no work to do inside. Shah Hussein was tall and well
built, an imposing man. "He thought if he was along, then I would
be okay if we ran into her family," Ali said. They set out in civvies
and had only just walked down the hill and turned in to the road
along the Kabul River (more an open-air sewer than a river, where
heroin addicts hang out under the bridges) in front of the Pamir
Cinema. Suddenly Ali heard someone shouting at him and turned
as Zakia's little brother, Razak, the nine-year-old, flung himself
at him, grabbing his lapels and screaming, "You kidnapper! You
eloper! Now you're finding out it's not so easy!" Ali pushed the boy
away only to see a policeman come up right behind him, leveling
an AK-47 assault rifle at him.

"Don't move. If you do, I'll kill you," the policeman said, adding,
as if to establish his credentials for violence, "I'm already answering
one charge for killing someone, so another one won't matter much."

Right behind him was Gula Khan. They had all been lying
in wait, probably staking out the neighborhood. The policeman
ordered his two prisoners to a guard shack nearby, and by then six
of Ali's male in-laws were all over Shah Hussein and Ali, manhan-
dling them and demanding to know Zakia's whereabouts, until
more police arrived and restored order. They were soon transferred
to the Police District 1 station house, where there was a lockup.

"The police wanted to know where she was, and I said in
Bamiyan," Ali told me. "I didn't care how much they beat me.
I wasn't going to confess and betray her." Her hiding place, as
he well knew, was only a couple hundred yards up the steep hill
nearby. The police said his father-in-law had accused him of kidnapping and murdering Zakia, and they wanted to know where
he'd dumped her body. Believing the worst, they beat him with

the butts of their rifles, then threw him into a cell and beat him some more in an effort to make him talk.

At some point Ali managed to pass his phone to his cousin, so that he would be able to call Anwar, Zakia, and Jawad, since Shah Hussein didn't have their numbers himself. After Zakia's relatives confirmed that Shah Hussein was not involved in the case, police freed him, but when he went outside the PD1 station, a gang of Zakia's relatives jumped him, beating him with bricks until he managed to run off. He regretted not having worn his uniform—they could never have treated him in public that way if he had. Once he was sure no one was following him, Shah Hussein climbed the hill to Ali's new house, but by the time he got there, Zakia and Anwar had fled; at Ali's aunt's house, his cousin changed into his uniform and went looking for them.

No one ever found out for sure how Zakia's family tracked them down, but some theories emerged. The extended family in Afghanistan is a powerful organization in its way and is normally so large, with relationships maintained over such a distant degree, that even the poorest family will have relatives far and wide, high and low. One of their distant relatives was a taxi driver, and before this whole affair he had driven Shah Hussein from Bamiyan to a house where Ali's aunt had previously lived. Although the aunt moved later, it was not far away from her previous home. That was Ali's theory anyway. Another possibility was that Shah Hussein, who had been meeting with Gula Khan and some of Zakia's cousins in an effort at reconciliation, might have been followed home. Anwar's theory was that someone had followed him down from the mountains when he came to town the week before. He'd had that creepy feeling that someone was following him, he said, though he could never spot anyone. My own theory? The aunt gave them up. Their relationship had soured, she was tired of being responsible for them, and she did not get along with her new niece. They had fortunately moved out of her house just before the capture, but it was to a place not far away, which would explain why the family had the neighborhood staked out, but not the actual house. Whatever the real explanation, it was a lesson in how hard it is to hide in Afghanistan, even in a city of 5 million people, many of them stuffed into dense slums. With its strong family networks, Afghan society is just not anonymous enough.

Zakia and Anwar's first stop was to the aunt's house, where Zakia borrowed a full-length *hejab,*[1] something she almost never wore. As a getaway costume, it was hard to beat; all that anyone could see were her eyes and her high-heeled shoes. The blue burqa would have been even better, but as Zakia often said, she wouldn't be caught dead in that thing. Anwar told his sister to take Zakia down into the city, and the two women wended their way between the mud masonry houses parallel to the river, high up on the hill. Zakia had no idea where anything was in Kabul and could not move around alone without arousing suspicion, so the sister agreed to help guide her, but she made it clear she was not happy about it. Anwar went straight down the steep path to the river.

"It was a difficult day for all of us," Jawad later said. "They kept calling me, calling me. 'What can you do for us?' Shah Hussein called me, Zakia called me. Anwar called me, and you could feel the pain and helplessness in his voice, and then he started crying, 'What should I do, what can I do?'"

Jawad called me again in Doha. "What should I tell them?"

"There's only one solution. You have to persuade them to take her to the shelter before the police find her. Have they left the house?"

"Yes."

"Why don't you meet them in your car, get them off the street, and drive around until they can decide what to do?"

Jawad agreed, and thus began a scramble in which the three of them tried for hours to find one another. Jawad still doesn't know if that was by accident, because they had such a poor knowledge of the city, or because Zakia and Anwar feared that he would somehow force them to put her in the shelter and therefore were avoiding him.

Zakia and Ali's aunt soon managed to meet up with Shah Hussein, who did know the city, and the aunt gratefully went home, leaving Zakia with Ali's cousin. "See what you have brought to us?" the aunt said on parting. Stepping out with Shah Hussein, however, was perilous enough in itself, because he was not proper *mahram* to Zakia—not a close enough male blood relative, or husband, to be allowed to escort her, although Ali had asked him to do that for them. Should they be arrested, those would be additional charges the police could bring: attempted *zina,* that novel Afghan offense of attempted adultery, in which a non-*mahram* couple are assumed to be on their way to have sex simply on the basis of their being alone in each other's company, even on a public street.

Complicating matters, Shah Hussein was under strict instructions from Ali, who had whispered them to him as his cousin left PD1: Take her back to the mountains and under no circumstances let her go to the WAW shelter. Zakia had relayed that message to Jawad, and for much of the day her only purpose in talking to him was to implore him to somehow use our supposed powers to get Ali out of prison. She refused to let Jawad come and pick her up, again because of the impropriety of being with an unrelated man. So Jawad concentrated on finding Anwar, thinking he could talk sense to Zakia, and also so she would have an acceptable *mahram* along. "He's an idiot. My son is stupid," Anwar said angrily in one of his many phone calls to Jawad. "Why was he going to a wedding? He never listens. How can I take her now? I don't have anyplace to go."

Jawad let the folks at WAW know what had happened, and the lawyer Shukria also called Zakia, trying to persuade her that going into the shelter was her only safe option as a woman alone and that it would not be the sort of prisonlike situation she had endured in Bamiyan.

At last Anwar told Jawad he was near a bridge across the Kabul River and there was a hospital nearby—that could only be the Ibn-Seena Hospital, so Jawad went there, parked in front of an abandoned police traffic kiosk on the bridge, and told Anwar where he could find him. Several calls later the old man climbed into his car. With Anwar along there was someone present who could be Zakia's *mahram,* so Jawad was able to persuade Zakia to let him pick her up, and she would be safely off the streets. He found her not far from the Allauddin Crossroads, in a Hazara neighborhood in western Kabul, standing beside the road with Shah Hussein, who was now in his full army uniform.

Zakia still wanted no part of the shelter. She removed her veil in the car, and her face was streaked with tears, slashing paths through her ruined makeup, mascara smeared to make raccoon eyes. "Let us go into the mountains, Uncle," she said to Anwar. She had taken to calling her father-in-law "uncle" as a token of affection and respect. He called her "daughter," as he had that first night she came into his home. He said okay, and they asked Jawad if he would take them to the edge of town. There was a minibus station there where they might find a late ride past the Paghman Mountain, which hems in the Kabul plateau from the west, and then into Bamiyan. That road was risky at night; the danger of the Taliban was compounded by the danger from Zakia's family, who might be lying in wait for them, knowing it was the most likely way for her to flee. Shah Hussein could not go with them; the next morning he had to report to duty, which he, unlike his cousin, took seriously, so it would just be Zakia and the old man. They would not be able to stay in Bamiyan city or their own village with the police looking for her; the authorities were no doubt alerted in Bamiyan as well that Ali had been arrested, and they would expect Zakia to go back to the valley.

Jawad was distressed at how upset Anwar seemed. "He looked so tired and beaten down." He realized that escaping into the mountains would mean they would have to leave cars and roads and climb, and he just felt too tired to do that. Their escape on the Shah Foladi mountain had nearly killed him, he felt, and he could not face it again. Still, he held his tongue and did not object overtly to Zakia's escape plan, except to say that he was worried about his high blood pressure. And, he added to Jawad, "Zakia is pregnant. She shouldn't be running in the mountains."

Zakia got the message that Anwar couldn't handle it; perhaps she felt the same way. She turned in her seat to face Anwar and spoke to him. She seemed quite calm and determined to be strong. "Uncle, don't worry about me. I'll be safe, and I'll stand by your side, and we will get the boy out. I will go to the shelter." Jawad could see that she was doing it for Anwar more than anything else; she knew that her husband wanted her to keep running, but she couldn't do that if it meant doing it without the old man or leaving him behind somewhere along the way.

Shukria had left her office at WAW and gone home, and reached there by phone at first she was reluctant to come out, but finally, in the middle of the night, she called the shelter. They sent her a minibus, and she rendezvoused with Jawad. Everyone piled into the minibus for the ride to the WAW shelter. Speaking quietly, Zakia kept reassuring her father-in-law that it would be all right. The gates of the shelter's compound swung open, the men dismounted, and the minibus drove in with just Zakia and Shukria. Jawad got his car and dropped Anwar off in a neighborhood where Anwar thought he might know someone. "I felt sorry for him," Jawad said. "He lost everything, he had no place to stay, his son was in jail, his daughter-in-law in the shelter, and they all thought this shelter was going to be like the one in Bamiyan and that she would be there for months and months." Jawad called Shah Hussein once more, to let him know where he had dropped his uncle. That phone did not ring, so he called Ali's phone, which Shah Hussein still had.

There was a new ringtone on it now, the song "Majnoon" by the Iranian singer Moein.

> In my soul I bear
> The pain and sorrow of your love:
> Do not let me wait any longer
> Watching for you by the roadside!
> I am crazy, I am possessed,
> Wild with love, I sing:
> I am Majnoon!
> Layli, without you
> I cannot live.[2]

"Zakia is in the shelter," Jawad told Shah Hussein. "Your uncle is safe." That night, though, Anwar would sleep on the street.

At the police station, Ali had been in for a rough time. As far as the police were concerned, he was at the very least a sex criminal for running away with a woman without her family's permission, quite possibly a kidnapper, and perhaps a murderer. "They beat me with rifle butts," he said. "Over and over until I grabbed the rifle butt and said, 'Please stop, you're not allowed to hurt me, and I'm just here because I love her and she loves me.'" The beatings stopped for a while, but he was refused food or the right to use the bathroom. Sharing a cell with four other men, he was obliged to soil himself and lie in the wet.

The next day detectives from the Criminal Investigation Division came to question him again, and he persisted with his story that Zakia had stayed in the mountains somewhere in Bamiyan and he had come alone to Kabul. "They didn't believe me. They already knew so much about my case," he said. Someone had been talking. They knew what house he had lived in with his aunt, that the couple had recently moved to another house nearby and where it was. Zakia and Anwar had been able to escape only because police bureaucracy had moved too slowly to follow up on Ali's arrest.

I suggested to Jawad that he go to the police station the next day, Saturday, to try to see Ali, while I wrote an article from Jawad's reporting about what had happened to the couple; there was just enough time to make the early deadlines for the Sunday bulldog (the print edition that comes out on Saturday afternoon), and I had a head start because I'd already written a tentative lede for just such a story when we'd begun to suspect both that Zakia was pregnant and that Ali would get caught.[3]

When Jawad and Anwar got to PD1, Zakia's family was there in force, hanging around outside the station, glowering and jeering at them as they walked past. At the lockup the jailers said that only the old man could visit his son, but this gave Jawad a chance to talk with the PD1 police chief, Colonel Jamila Bayaz. She was famous as the first female police chief of an Afghan police district.[4] I had interviewed her when she was appointed earlier in the year; it was something the Ministry of Interior liked to boast about,[5] since the lack of female officers,[6] especially in key positions, was

an issue that was important to the international community. I had
heard that Colonel Bayaz was quite good—later in 2014 she was
promoted to brigadier general, one of only four female general officers in the Ministry of Interior and its police agencies at the time.
There had been a fifth one, in charge of gender issues, Brigadier
General Shafiqa Quraishi, but she fled the country and sought asylum abroad.[7] During my earlier interview with Colonel Bayaz, her
deputy, a man, a senior official who wouldn't be named, another
man, and two or three other policemen all crowded into the room.
When I asked Jamila questions, they answered for her. "As things
like my promotion happen, it motivates other women to do more,"
she said when she managed to get a word in edgewise on her own
interview. She did say something else, though, quite unbidden and,
as it would later turn out, quite plaintive. "I am sure our international friends will not abandon us," she said. I later learned, from
Western diplomats in Kabul, that she had applied to the Canadian
government for asylum.[8]

At the time of Ali's arrest, though, Colonel Bayaz had been on
the job for six months and was earning a reputation as a tough advocate for better treatment of women by the police, and she seemed
very much in charge of her station. Jawad found her sympathetic to
Zakia and Ali's story—although unaware of Ali's mistreatment in
her lockup by the detectives (she was in direct charge of the uni-
formed officers only). "I know it's a love story and the boy eloped
with a girl who loved him. Higher-level officials have told me,
'Please make sure he doesn't escape.'" As everyone in Afghanistan
well knows, escapes from Afghan lockups and prisons are routine
and not very expensive, an opportunity for guards to supplement
their incomes.

No one was more aware of that than Zakia's family members,
on their stakeout of the district police station. "We know you want
to bribe that woman police chief to get him out, but we're not
going to let you," Zaman told Anwar as he came out. "We have
friends, too, you'll see."

Shukria came to the police station later that day, carrying a
signed statement from Zakia that she had not been kidnapped. The

bigamy charges had gone away—perhaps her family did not feel they could make that charge stick, although they were still claiming she was married to a cousin she had never met. Or perhaps the attorney general's office just didn't believe the bigamy charge, since the judges in Bamiyan had themselves attested that Zakia was engaged, not married—and breaking an engagement is a civil matter, not a criminal one. But the detectives handling the case were not interested in the fine points Shukria presented to them; they were treating it as a criminal kidnapping offense, and they deemed an exculpatory letter from Ali's wife and supposed victim insufficient.

For a second day, Ali said, he was beaten by officers and denied food and use of the toilet. Later in the day, he was moved along with some of the other detainees into a steaming-hot shipping container that served as their temporary jail cell due to overcrowding in the PD1 lockup. "We were five people in the container, and they brought a crane in to move the container to another place."

"Don't you want to take these detainees out first?" the crane engineer asked the detective in charge.

"No, these people are criminals and not to be considered human. Just move the container with them inside it."

The prisoners were just banged up a little, but for a terrifying few minutes they thought Kabul was being destroyed in an earthquake. Afterward Ali would always think of this ordeal whenever he had to move a birdcage with a quail or a canary inside. Nothing is more unsettling than a prison that moves, with the inmates having no idea where they're going.

Ali was philosophical about his rough treatment by the policemen at the PD1 lockup. "Life is not easy for any of us. I've undergone a lot of hardship, but I care about my life." Regarding his tormenter, he said, "Perhaps he is a person who doesn't care much about his life. Perhaps he just doesn't love his wife. He might have married someone he didn't love. It could be that his father or mother forced him to marry his wife. I am thankful to God that I don't have that problem."

At the time, though, Ali thought his life was over. Zakia

thought her life was over. Anwar was sure that their life together, at least, was over.

I was relieved. Now the couple had no choice but to let Women for Afghan Women take their case to court. Once they were no longer fugitives from the law, they could easily get passports. Also, Zakia was safe. Her pregnancy was no great surprise; we'd been hearing that she was sick on this or that day or off to the hospital because of nausea—the usual sort of first-trimester complaints. Like most Afghans, Zakia and Ali were not interested in family planning, unless by that one means planning a very large family. Ali had laughed when we asked him if they wanted children. "I don't mind. Yeah, why not? A person has to have children for when he dies, so someone will remember him." Under different circumstances we might not have found out so soon. Pregnancy is not something many Afghan couples are willing to divulge outside the family, especially when it doesn't show, but Anwar had accidentally confirmed it in the excitement of the night before. Now Juliet was with child and her Romeo was in jail, indirectly in the figurative clutches of the Capulets and their sympathizers. If that was not going to win the lovers some serious support, in and out of Afghanistan, perhaps nothing ever would.

❧

# 10

# RELUCTANT CELEBRITIES

It was a variation on the riddle of whether a falling tree makes a sound if there is no one in the forest to hear it: Could Zakia and Ali really be celebrities if they scarcely knew about their celebrity? What could modern celebrity possibly mean to someone who had never used a personal computer or gone on the Internet? Who could not read or write, had never watched television, and did not own a radio? Who in short was unplugged from electronic society (the single exception being cell phones, which they only partly knew how to use)? Many Afghans now saw the couple as celebrities; nearly every Afghan radio and television station and newspaper covered their capture, especially the Dari outlets, and young Afghans began starting Facebook pages and Twitter campaigns in their support. Jawad was besieged by Afghan journalists who were enlisted by the BBC or *60 Minutes,* or Australian, Canadian, and German television to cover the story. But locked up without cell phones, Zakia and Ali had little idea of the storm of attention building around their predicament.

At Women for Afghan Women, Shukria was working hard to

find a resolution to their case, and because she had already started working on it before Ali's arrest, she was well along. Her first legal move was to petition the attorney general's office to move the case to family court, as a dispute between families, not a criminal case. Then she worked out an arrangement for the police to come to WAW's shelter to interview Zakia. "They won't arrest her and take her to the detention center," Manizha Naderi of WAW said. "They will allow her to stay in the shelter until she's convicted in court. And we won't let that happen. Fingers crossed!"

In the meantime Zakia had plenty to say and was widely quoted; WAW was only too happy to arrange interviews, because Manizha sees public outreach and education as a vital part of her organization's mission.[1] Under the circumstances, speaking out seemed to Zakia the natural thing to do, and she was no longer afraid of the sound of her own voice, although she would have been surprised if anyone had tried to explain to her how famous she and Ali had become. "I am by his side, and at court I will say no one kidnapped me, that I came by my consent and will, and I want to be with him for the rest of my life," Zakia said. "If I see my father and brothers, I will tell them, 'Whatever has happened, has happened, and it is nothing you can change. Why is it any of your business that this has happened? This has just happened. You cannot change what's in my heart, so stop trying to do anything about it.'"

She was still worried about her family's retribution. "If I fell into my parents' hands, they will do something to me, kill me or something else even worse. There is nothing they want to do except to kill me. I haven't even seen my aunt's son—how is it possible that I would have been married to him? There was no *neka*. How is it possible? I said this to my father and asked them, 'Why do you lie?' But if it is left to my father and mother, they will not agree with me even in ten years." Mostly, though, she was worried about Ali and about her father-in-law. "He is ill and has high blood pressure, and he must be very worried. They have to let the boy go, that is all."

Zakia's father, Zaman, was stunned by the onslaught of interest about his daughter's case. Nothing could be more galling to a potential honor killer than the glare of publicity. Zaman had soon adjusted his narrative to the prevailing mood.

"My young son"—this would have been Razak—"saw him and went to the police and told the police this person has done this crime, he kidnapped my daughter. What can we do? If we *could* do something, we *would* do something. I am a poor person and don't have the power to harm anyone. What can I do? If I was a rich and powerful person, I would do something. No one is listening to me. If I would kill him, everyone would blame me for it. But you see, we handed him to the police." That was true, but it was Zakia they most wanted. They had hoped Ali would lead the authorities and hence her family to Zakia. There is not all that much honor in killing the offending man, since a man is just seen as doing what men do, whether it's seduction or even rape. It is the death of the woman that is required by this concept of honor.

"The police asked me to come and give a statement, and I went and did that," Zaman said. "I told them what that boy has done. He kidnapped my daughter. Isn't that true? We want the girl back, and we want to hand her to her husband and see what he does with her." He meant his nephew, the supposed husband by Zakia's first marriage, which she never attended. "The boy we married Zakia to has made claims against me. He spent a lot of money, and he wants it back or he wants his wife back. All I want is that the girl should be handed to her first husband. Then it is up to him whether he accepts her as his wife or not. If that doesn't work, I will leave it to God. I can't do anything myself. I lost everything and came here to Kabul with fifteen family members, and we're all working on the streets."

The police were in no hurry to interview Zakia at the shelter, so Shukria went to the Ministry of Interior on Sunday and won permission for Ali's criminal case to be dismissed if she could produce Zakia to swear that Ali had not kidnapped her and that they were married. She and three WAW staffers took Zakia to PD1, the police station, and Zakia made her declaration; they managed to get her in and out by a side entrance to avoid her family. When Shukria later went back to PD1 to tell Ali how things were going, Zakia's father and uncle saw her. They blocked her way and demanded the right to visit Zakia at the WAW shelter. Shukria agreed they could visit in a couple of days, after they had calmed down. They were so angry that it was clear to her that they would kill either the girl or Ali on sight.

"Stop shouting at me!" she told the men, shouting back at them. "You will never see her without my permission, and you will never get that permission unless you calm down and behave with respect." Never having been really yelled at by a woman, particularly one who exuded authority, Zakia's relatives were easily cowed—for the moment.

After Zakia and Shukria's visit, the police accepted that they no longer had a criminal case but instead a family dispute. Ali soon saw a difference in the way he was treated. The beatings stopped; he was given food and allowed to use the toilet facilities. "They even offered me cigarettes," he said. He had quit smoking at Zakia's request after they arrived in Kabul; this was the first time he'd broken his vow to her.

The day after their encounter with Shukria, Zakia's family began fighting back. Her father and her brother Gula Khan showed up in the WAW offices as part of the entourage of a high official from the Ministry of Interior, who introduced himself as a director general, a department head of some sort. He never produced a name, but he demanded to know why the *New York Times* had delivered Zakia to the shelter and what the paper's role in the whole matter was. "We know that the *New York Times* brought the girl here, and why did they do that? We know that the U.S. embassy and the *New York Times* helped the girl and the boy and support them." Behind him, Zaman and his sons, emboldened by having a powerful man in their midst, were screaming at Shukria and the other women present, demanding to get in to see Zakia. Shukria stood her ground, told the official she had no idea what he was talking about, and made sure that WAW's guards kept the visitors from the living quarters of the shelter itself.

Then Zaman had a lawyer petition to move the case from a civil proceeding in family court to the attorney general's office, as

**Dead Father's Daughter:** Zakia's family came from Kham-e-Kalak village, Bamiyan Province, adjoining Surkh Dar, where donkeys were their only form of transport. (*Quilty*)

**Under the Gaze of the Buddhas:** The Bamiyan Valley from the vantage point of the Great Buddha Solsal, photographed from inside the niche where the Buddha's head had been. The shelter in Bamiyan from which Zakia escaped is on the upper plateau at the foot of the brown foothills in the center. (*Sánchez*)

**Honor Hunters:** Zakia's father, Zaman, with three of his younger children at his home in Kham-e-Kalak, before he moved to Kabul to hunt down his daughter. (*Lima*)

**"If you love me, I also love you":** Ali's father, Mohammad Anwar. (*Sánchez*)

**Mystery Benefactor:** Fatima Kazimi, then the head of the ministry of women's affairs in Bamiyan Province, who rescued Zakia from her family and later fled Afghanistan, successfully winning asylum in the United States for helping the lovers. (*Lima*)

**Dead Father's Daughter:** The first *New York Times* portrait of Zakia, February 2014, while she was still held in the Bamiyan shelter. (*Lima*)

**A Beautiful Place to Hide:** The home of Zahra and Haji Abdul Hamid in Kham-e Bazargan, where Zakia and Ali twice hid while fleeing. (*Sánchez*)

**Zakia Makes Her Move:** This picture of Zakia and Ali on the run, first published in the *New York Times*, has become iconic, with many Afghan artists painting versions of it. (*Sánchez*)

**Where did they ever get this idea?** Holding hands is not something often done in Afghanistan, even among married couples and especially not in public. (*Sánchez*)

**The Irreconcilables:** The Chindawul neighborhood in Kabul, where the couple hid until Ali's arrest. In this view, the Pamir Cinema building is the pale yellow building in the foreground; Ali was captured nearby. (*Quilty*)

**Mullah Mohammad Jan:** Anwar and Ali prepare for their flight to Tajikistan, buying suitcases at a marketplace in Kabul. (*Sukhanyar*)

BELOW **Honor Hunters:** Ali's father, Anwar, near the Kabul River the day after his son was arrested. He had no idea where to go, and no place to stay. (*Quilty*)

**A Dog with No Name:** The compound of Anwar's house in Surkh Dar, with the new guard dog chained outside. (*Quilty*)

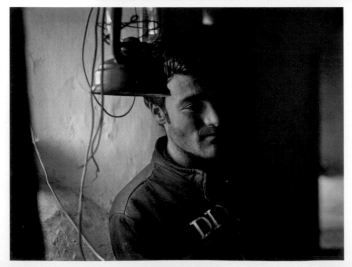

ABOVE **"We have our proof"**: Ali's mother, Chaman; Zakia with Ruqia, age two months; and Ali, February 2015. (*Quilty*)

LEFT **"She can smell her family in the air"**: Ali, in the family home in Surkh Dar, still in hiding well into 2015. (*Quilty*)

"He is still nervous when he holds her": Ali with his daughter, Ruqia, at his father's house in the village of Surkh Dar, in September 2015. (*Hayeri*)

"Whatever happens, we had this time together": Zakia and Ruqia, at home in Ali's father's house in Surkh Dar village, Bamiyan, in September 2015, eighteen months after the lovers eloped. (*Hayeri*)

"Now they will all go to school": Ali's parents, Anwar and Chaman, at home with their newest grandchild, Ruqia, in September 2015. (*Hayeri*)

**Birds in a Cage:** Ali trapping quail in the family fields; he keeps birdsongs on his cell phone. (*Quilty*)

**"Enmity like this they will never give up":** Ali working the fields, armed and ready, in February 2015. (*Quilty*).